Birkenhead Railways
A PHOTOGRAPHIC HISTORY

Birkenhead Railways

A PHOTOGRAPHIC HISTORY

Merseyside Railway History Group

Lightmoor Press

The original wooden bodied Mersey Railway stock lasted until BR days in a drab green livery and a set enters Birkenhead Park station in its last year in July 1956. The leading driving motor bears white plates between the windows denoting First Class accommodation. *David Kelso*

Preface to the Merseyside Railway History Group

The MRHG was formed in 1977 and comprises railway enthusiasts interested in the history of local and national railways from their origins to the present day. The group has previously published five books on local railways: -

- The Hooton to West Kirby Branch Line and the Wirral Way (1982).
- Railway stations of the Wirral (1994).
- The Last Merseyrail Signal Boxes and their Heritage, Part1 The Wirral Line (2004)
- The Last Merseyrail Signal Boxes and their Heritage, Part 2 The Northern Line (2006).
- Chester Railways (2015)

Monthly meetings are held presenting a variety of railway related topics between September and April at the United Reform Church in West Kirby. Further details can be obtained from the group's website at mrhg.org.

MRHG BOOKS are produced by a special sub group and those responsible for this publication are:
Ian Anderson, Adrian Bodlander, John Cowlishaw, Jon Penn and David Southern.

Introduction

This publication arose from a suggestion made at one of the MRHG meetings, shortly after the release of the last book in 2015. As we had covered Chester to Mollington it was thought a good idea to carry on the journey to Birkenhead Woodside but also include the docks which provided such a great amount of goods traffic.

The book takes two journeys; the first starting off where the Chester book finished, just north of the site of Mollington station, to Birkenhead North Junction including branches and the docks. The second, a journey on Merseyrail from Rock Ferry via Hamilton Square, again finishing at Birkenhead North Junction close to the current Merseyrail depot. All aspects of the railway scene have been covered in the form of stations, goods yards, locomotive sheds and ships in the docks.

Acknowledgements

The authors are very conscious that this publication Birkenhead Railways - A Photographic History would not have been possible without the support of a number of people. First and foremost are the photographers who have recorded the railway scene around Birkenhead from the 19th century to the present day. Wherever possible they have been credited individually but in a number of cases the name of the individual photographer has been lost over time.

In these cases the name of the individual or organisation holding the copy of the print or postcard has been credited. Particular mention must be made of Ted Lloyd, Jon Penn, members of the Hambly family and Pacer Archive who have allowed access to their collections. Thanks to Barry Shore for the proof reading of the text. Finally thanks must go to the families of the authors who have tolerated numerous meetings and to Adrian Bodlander for the refreshments provided.

CONTENTS

Preface, Introduction, Acknowledgements

CHAPTER ONE... PAGE 7
The Joint Line - GWR and L&NWR - Mollington to Birkenhead Woodside
* MOLLINGTON NORTH * CAPENHURST * LEDSHAM * HOOTON * EASTHAM RAKE *
* BROMBOROUGH * BROMBOROUGH RAKE * SPITAL * PORT SUNLIGHT (LEVER BROS) * BEBINGTON & NEW FERRY *
* ROCK FERRY * GREEN LANE JUNCTION * BIRKENHEAD MOLLINGTON STREET MOTIVE POWER DEPOT *
* MONKS FERRY * BLACKPOOL STREET * BIRKENHEAD TOWN * BIRKENHEAD WOODSIDE *

CHAPTER TWO... PAGE 87
Birkenhead Docks Extension Railway
* BIRKENHEAD FLYOVERS * THE SOUGH * BROOK STREET *

CHAPTER THREE... PAGE 93
Birkenhead Docks
* SHORE STREET * SHORE ROAD ENGINE SHED * MORPETH DOCK * FOUR BRIDGES * EGERTON DOCK *
* CANNING STREET NORTH *

CHAPTER FOUR... PAGE 115
Mersey Docks And Harbour Board - The 'Cross-Dock' Route
* CATHCART STREET GOODS DEPOT * VITTORIA DOCK * DUKE STREET * CAVENDISH WHARF *
* CAVENDISH SIDINGS * BEAUFORT ROAD *

CHAPTER FIVE... PAGE 137
Mersey And Wirral Railways - Rock Ferry to Birkenhead North
* ROCK FERRY * GREEN LANE * BIRKENHEAD CENTRAL * HAMILTON SQUARE * CONWAY PARK *
* BIRKENHEAD PARK * BIRKENHEAD NORTH * BIRKENHEAD NORTH LOCOMOTIVE SHED *
* BIRKENHEAD NORTH ELECTRIC DEPOT *

© Lightmoor Press and the author
Designed by Mike Day

British Library Cataloguing-in-Publication Data.
A catalogue record for this book is available from the British Library
ISBN: 9 781915 069030
All rights reserved. No part of this publication may be reproduced, stored in a retrieval system or transmitted in any form or by any means, electronic, mechanical, photocopying, recording or otherwise, without the written permission of the publisher.

LIGHTMOOR PRESS
Unit 144B, Lydney Trading Estate, Harbour Road, Lydney, Gloucestershire GL15 5EJ
www.lightmoor.co.uk
Lightmoor Press is an imprint of Black Dwarf Lightmoor Publications Ltd

Printed in Poland
www.lfbookservices.co.uk

MOLLINGTON NORTH

Photographs in this book commence north of the site of Mollington station at Demage Lane overbridge, where royal liveried No. 67005 *Royal Messenger* is at the rear of the 06.40 Shrewsbury to Edinburgh 'The Waverley Express' on 12th April 2012. This locomotive would be used to haul the train after its reversal at Hooton to proceed via Ellesmere Port; No. 67027 *Rising Star* was at the front of the train. *John Cowlishaw*

Chapter One
THE JOINT LINE – GWR AND L&NWR
Mollington to Birkenhead Woodside

Following the opening of the Liverpool & Manchester Railway in 1830 there were a number of proposals for a railway to connect Birkenhead and Chester. Several were unsuccessful before the Chester & Birkenhead Railway was incorporated by an Act of Parliament on 12th July 1837 and opened between Chester and Grange Lane (Birkenhead) on 23rd September 1840. This line was amalgamated with the Lancashire & Cheshire Junction Railway, which had a line from Chester to Walton Junction (Warrington) with running powers to Manchester, to form the Birkenhead Railway.

After various disagreements with both the L&NWR and GWR, the Birkenhead Railway was transferred jointly to the GWR and L&NWR on 1st January 1860 and under full control by them on 20th November 1860. Until nationalisation of the railways in 1948 the line was run by a joint committee.

The Birkenhead Railway was standard gauge and at last gave the Great Western Railway access to Birkenhead Docks and tenuously to Liverpool. A branch from Hooton to Parkgate opened on 1st October 1866 and later extended to West Kirby on 19th April 1886. Grange Lane the original Birkenhead terminus was replaced on 23rd October 1844 by Monks Ferry, approached by a single track tunnel, as the first riverside terminus. Eventually it became too small for the traffic so Woodside station was opened on 31st March 1878, 400 yards to the north and located next to the ferry terminal to Liverpool.

Birkenhead Docks was served by the Birkenhead Docks Extension Railway which diverged from the Chester & Birkenhead line just before Birkenhead Town station, and passed through the centre of Birkenhead in a walled cutting known as 'The Sough' before reaching the dock lines at Canning Street. This line opened on 1st April 1847 at the same time as the docks in Birkenhead. The L&NWR, GWR, GC and CLC all had goods yards in the dock estate connected to the dock lines; the CLC also had a small locomotive shed at Shore Road.

Improvements to the line included quadrupling between Ledsham Junction and Blackpool Street in Birkenhead, to cater for the increasing freight traffic at the turn of the last century. A line from Hooton to

BR standard tank No. 82033 calls at Capenhurst on 7th August 1958 with a Birkenhead bound train. Worthy of note are the substantial station buildings and well maintained gardens. Capenhurst station was opened in 1870 on land donated by Captain Hope Jones and Mr Shawcross, as the railway had refused to build one four years earlier. *H.B.Priestly/Pacer Archives*

Helsby was built and at Rock Ferry an interchange was created with the Mersey Railway, providing a service to Liverpool under the river. North of Rock Ferry a large steam shed was built jointly by the GWR and L&NWR at Mollington Street with extensive sidings at Blackpool Street/Grange Lane opposite. Birkenhead Town station was then built near the site of the original terminus of Grange Lane. Large industrial companies had connections from the Birkenhead Railway for example, Cammell Laird's shipyard, and Lever Brother's soap works at Port Sunlight and Bromborough Dock, with nearly all the stations having small goods yards.

With British Railways came rationalisation, closing the Hooton to West Kirby line to passenger traffic on 17th September 1956 and completely on 7th May 1962. The line from Ledsham Junction to Rock Ferry was reduced to two tracks due to loss of freight and the closure of Birkenhead Woodside on 4th November 1967 with services truncated to Rock Ferry. In the 1970s Merseyrail electrics were extended with a loop line under the centre of Liverpool, and the Rock Ferry to Chester and Ellesmere Port lines electrified in the 1980/90s. Since 1993 the goods lines to the docks have been abandoned out of use, are partially severed and completely overgrown.

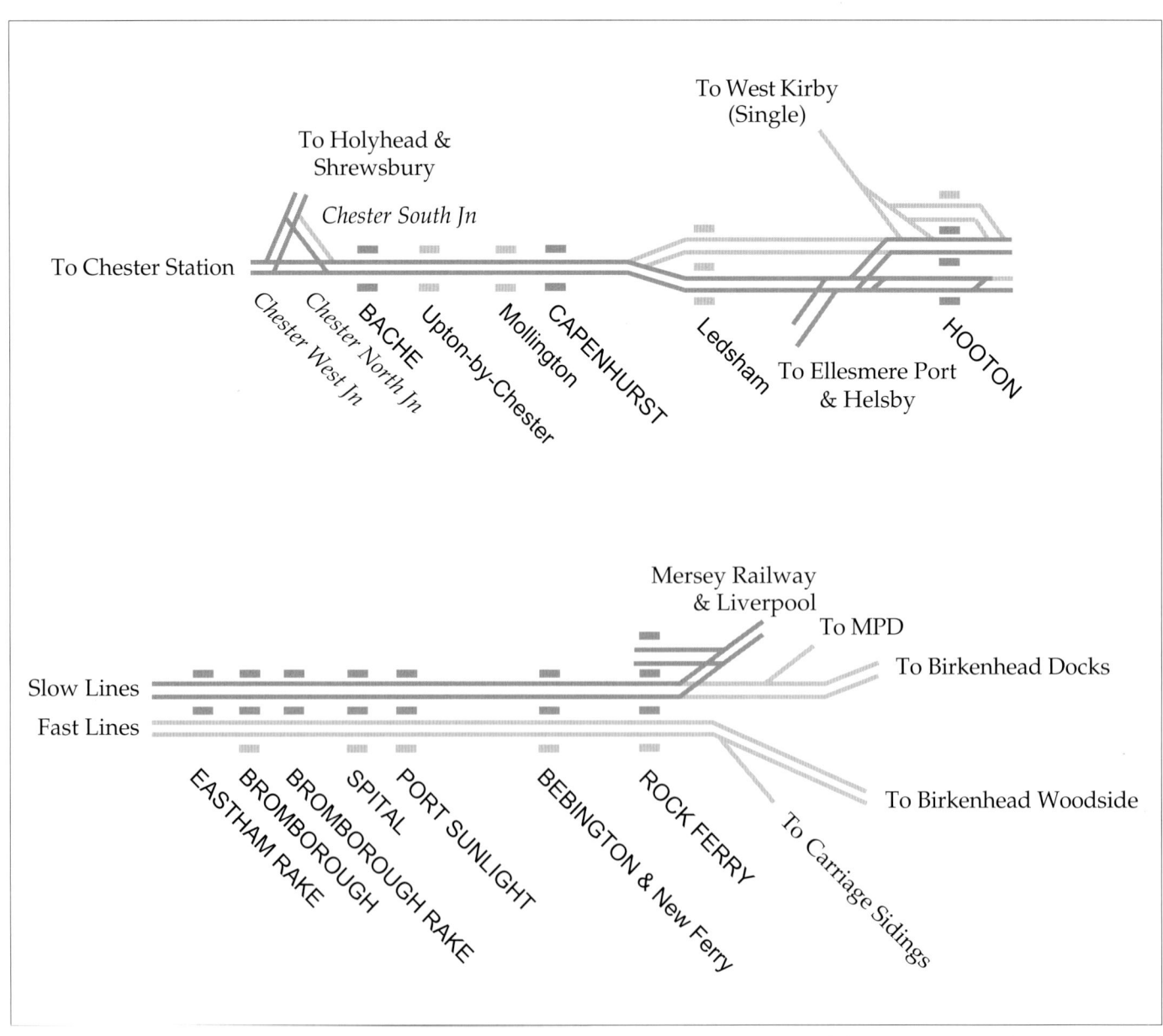

The Great Western and London & North Western Joint Railway ran from Chester to Birkenhead and this diagram shows the arrangement of lines and stations, with closed lines shown in light grey and the current lines in a darker shade

Also on 7th August 1958 Pannier Tank No. 9728 passes southbound through Capenhurst with a train of vans. A prominent feature is the telegraph pole route with twin poles supporting seven crossbars. The station was unusual in not having goods facilities, with the signal box located to the north serving the sidings on the down side and a small up loop. *H.B.Priestly/Pacer Archives*

In the late evening on 21st July 2006, No. 67028 heads south though Capenhurst with the 20.20 Hooton to Rugby special in connection with the Open Golf Championship played at the Royal Liverpool Course at Hoylake; No. 67017 was at the rear of the train. The station buildings had been demolished with only waiting shelters provided.
John Cowlishaw

Ledsham Junction signal box was located about a mile south of Ledsham station and controlled the transition between the two-track and four-track sections. Looking north, the fast lines are on the right and the slow lines are on the left. Both were speed restricted with the fast lines having a 50 mph limit and the slow lines down to 20 mph. In 1904 the 14 miles north of Ledsham Junction were quadrupled, but the lines south were not as the engineering difficulties were greater. This southern section contained the largest structure on the line, the Moston Viaduct over the Shropshire Union Canal. The signal box contained a twenty lever L&NWR tumbler frame and survived until 24th August 1972, by which time most of the slow lines had been removed.
Jon Penn Collection

Shunting a short freight train LMS Class '2P' 4-4-0 No. 40658, resident at Chester in the 1950s, stands on the down slow line south of Ledsham station. With the signalman's bicycle under the steps Ledsham Station signal box is prominent in the foreground. This closed on 11th October 1959 and was replaced by an electrically released ground frame to control access to the residual siding.

H.B.Priestly/Pacer Archives

Ledsham station in the 1910s looking towards Chester and the entrance off Ledsham lane. The style of building leading to the footbridge is the same as Bromborough and Spittal stations further north. The high co-acting platform starting signals are visible for approaching trains with Ledsham Junction distant signals located beneath the stop arm. *Michael Day*

A Great Western Pannier Tank, probably No. 9728, passes through Ledsham in the 1950s with a freight bound for Chester. Of note are the different styles of gas lamps on the station, while the fields and trees beyond the station show the rural nature of the location. Ledsham station opened in 1840 and closed on 20th July 1959.

I Vaughan

Taken from Heath Lane Bridge EMU No. 507016 in the distinctive Merseyrail yellow and black livery, approaches Hooton in 1997 with a Liverpool bound train. The extension of electrified services to Chester commenced in October 1993. The open land to the left is the trackbed of the former slow lines, with the former fast lines being those in use today in this section. In the distance Hooton station can be seen and the junction with the Ellesmere Port / Helsby line diverging to the right. *David Southern*

HOOTON

A Class '101' DMU arrives in the bay platform at Hooton, from Helsby and Ellesmere Port in 1985. In the distance is Hooton signal box and in front its replacement, a two-storey modular building. To the left of the signal box is the junction for the Helsby line. The roof of the former goods shed can be seen above the train.
David Southern

The impressive Hooton signal box; originally named Hooton South Junction contained a 128 L&NWR tumbler lever frame to control this busy location. Later it reduced to 80 levers as traffic declined and the layout simplified. Most boxes on the joint line were provided by the L&NWR after transfer of signalling responsibility from the GWR in 1885, with Mackenzie & Holland being the signalling contractor. This box closed in 1985 and was replaced by a modular building as shown in the next photograph.
Edgar Richards/Jon Penn Collection

The replacement signal box was a modular building to the south of the station, housing the new Hooton Power Box controlling the much simplified layout. This opened in 1985 as part of the third rail extension from Rock Ferry to Hooton. A Pacer No. 142030, is seen passing the box with a train for Helsby in the late 1980s. *David Southern*

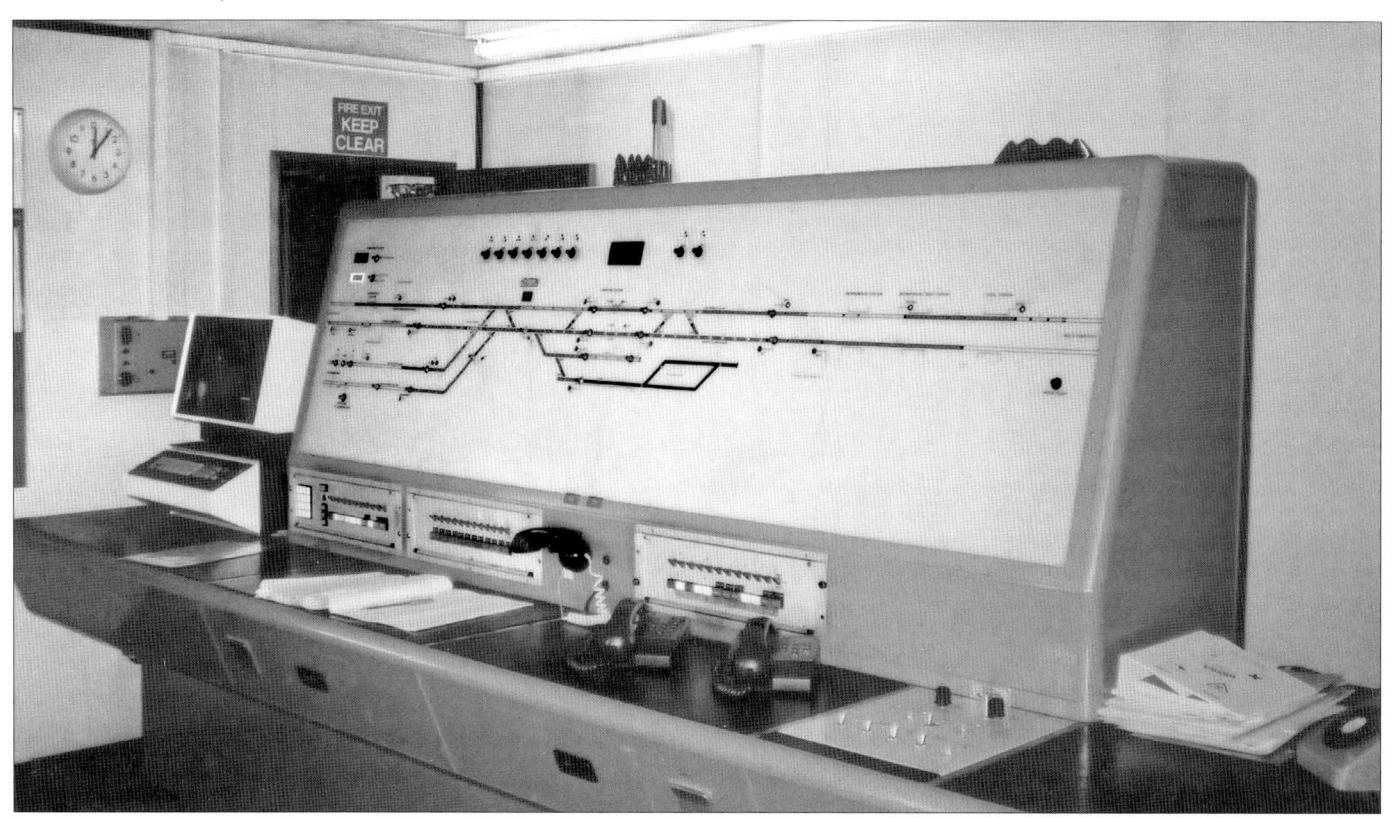

An interior view of Hooton Power Box showing the operating panel of the NX (entrance/exit) type with a much reduced track layout. The main line has two tracks heading right (north) towards Birkenhead with the Helsby branch joining at the lower left of the panel. The bay platform and freight loop are in the centre of the diagram. The small VDU screen to the left of the panel is a train describer. This 'temporary' signal box continued in use for 28 years until 11th November 2013, when control of the Hooton area was transferred to Chester Power Box. *David Southern*

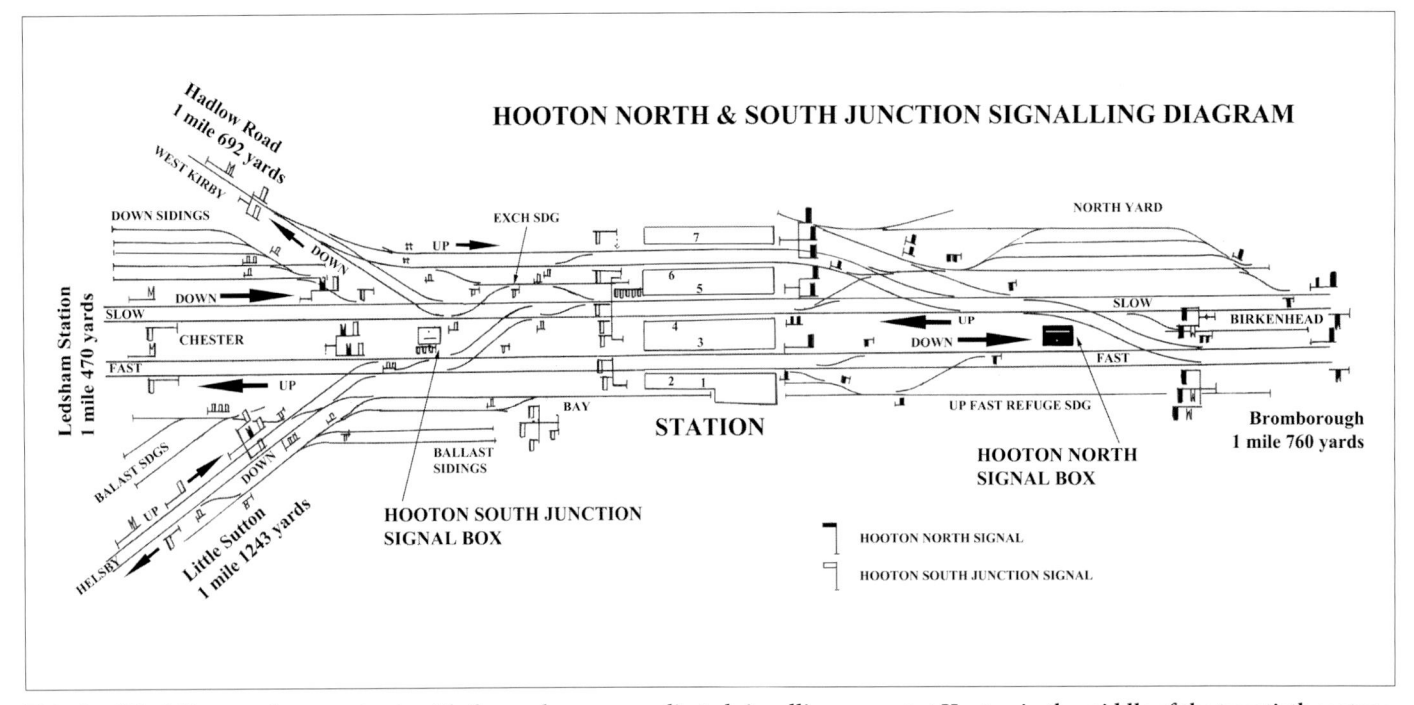

HOOTON NORTH & SOUTH JUNCTION SIGNALLING DIAGRAM

This simplified diagram above contrasts with the much more complicated signalling present at Hooton in the middle of the twentieth century. The diagram shows the signalling for both Hooton North & Hooton South Junction signal boxes, with signals worked by the North box shown solid and those by the South box in outline.

The West Kirby branch leads away to the top left of the diagram and the line to Helsby and Ellesmere Port to the bottom left. Note on both of these branches the up and down directions were different to the main lines through Hooton station, where the convention of London bound lines being 'up' was used. These days under Merseyrail the directions have been reversed from Hooton northwards to accord with the Mersey Railways designation of 'up' heading towards Liverpool.

Pacer unit No. 142030 in Regional Railways livery departs from the truncated fast line platform at Hooton with a train for Helsby. The photograph was taken from the power box and shows the newly laid track switching the main running lines from the previous fast lines to the slow lines through the station. The land occupied by the former goods shed and adjacent field had by then been transformed into a large 'Park & Ride' car park. *David Southern*

A chlorine tank train destined for the Associated Octel Co. at Amlwch on the Isle of Anglesey, hauled by No. 40004 leaves Hooton in 1983. The locomotive has run round its train after arriving from Ellesmere Port to proceed to Chester and the North Wales coast; a brake van and barrier wagon were provided at each end of the train to facilitate this. This working lasted until 1993.
David Southern

The goods shed on 7th March 1937, the water tank having now been removed and extra tracks added to serve the goods shed. The many pipes on the right were part of the borehole and pumping station located on Waterworks Lane. Numerous private owner wagons stand alongside the shed, while some rails and other permanent way items are stacked on the wooden decking, including spare sections for points. The very tall posts at the end of the platforms were needed to make the signals visible for approaching trains above the bridges. *J.A.Peden/IRS*

GWR 'Large Prairie' 2-6-2T No. 4120 waits in the bay platform with the 3.05 pm train for Helsby on 20th April 1954. The box van on the adjacent siding is being unloaded onto a waiting lorry. *H.C.Casserley*

An overall view of Hooton station taken from the South Junction signal box in the early 1920s, with the original very tall platform starting signals visible. From left to right the tracks are the down and up West Kirby, the down and up slow, down and up fast and the Helsby bay. The goods shed on the right was an engine shed in the nineteenth century, hence the adjacent water tank. A passenger train on the up fast has been given the road for Chester, whilst another can be seen shunting in the Helsby bay. The signals on the slow line to the left had rings denoting goods lines but these were removed from 1926 onwards.
John Ryan Collection

On Wednesday 2nd August 1961 Stanier 'Mogul' No. 42981 arrives at Hooton, in charge of the 9.30 am Bournemouth to Birkenhead train, which it will have taken over at Chester. The train started behind Southern motive power to Oxford, where a local 'Castle' Class locomotive took over for the run to Chester via Shrewsbury. Upon reversal at Chester the Castle and some coaches were detached and the reduced consist (to fit in Woodside station) worked forward up the Wirral by Midland power. The stock on the service alternated each day between Midland and Southern types; this picture showing the latter with the set number 427 prominent on the leading coach. By this date the catering facilities on this train had reduced to Saturdays only. Standing in the Helsby Bay platform is classmate 42969, also allocated to Birkenhead, waiting to leave with the 6.07 pm all stations to Liverpool Lime Street via Helsby and Runcorn. The platform starting signals on both lines are fitted with shortened arms to be more visible for southbound trains under the bridge at the north end of the station.

J.A.Peden/IRS

On 30th September 1985 the third rail electric system was extended from Rock Ferry to Hooton and to mark the occasion one of the Class '503' EMUs, dating from 1938, was restored to its original maroon livery. These units were designed by the London Midland & Scottish Railway (LMS) and included the then new concept of air operated sliding doors controlled by the guard. Further sets were built for British Railways in 1956 to the same design. Both types were built by Metro-Cammell of Saltley in Birmingham who supplied the motor coaches, and Birmingham RC&W of Smethwick built the underframes. They had four position front marker lights with two top lights indicating Rock Ferry services. The central doors at the unit ends were introduced in 1972 to provide emergency egress for running in the forthcoming single track tunnels of the Liverpool Loop line. *David Southern*

LMS '*Crab*' No. 42942 has been smartened up for the 'Hundred of Wirral' railtour on 6th August 1966, organised by the L.C.G.B. & Branch Line Society using nine brake vans. It ran from Birkenhead Woodside to Mold Junction, Helsby, Mickle Trafford, Dee Marsh and Bidston. *Brian Taylor*

A Class '47' passes through Hooton with a train of empty Grainflow wagons from Birkenhead to March in Cambridgeshire. The grain was delivered to various flour mills located around Birkenhead Docks from East Anglia. The bright insulators on the third rail indicate that the picture was taken after electrification extension to Hooton but before the L&NWR signal box closed. The prominent covered footbridge is visible in this view; before the West Kirby platforms became disused, the footbridge originally continued for a third span to the left. The footbridge was replaced by a much larger example with lifts around 2015.
Transport Topics

In July 1955 GWR 2-6-2 'Tank' No. 4122 takes water at Hooton while working a Birkenhead bound train. The fireman struggles to hold the 'bag', with the driver standing by the water valve, and a family down the ramp in the company of a waist-coated porter, probably with a pram wanting to use the barrow crossing at the platform end
John Ryan Collection

'Stanier Prairie' tanks, No's 40110 and 40135, are seen alongside the water columns at the north end of Hooton station both heading north in the mid 1950s. On the fast line No. 40110 is taking water and has a consist including Great Western coaches befitting the joint nature of the line. Note the 'fire devil' alongside the nearest column complete with coal, ash and shovel. *Transport Treasury*

GWR 'Dean Metro' 2-4-0T No. 1495 stands in platform 2 at Hooton with an autocoach, sometime before it received a Belpaire firebox in 1917. The 'Metro' Class name arose from their initial use over the Metropolitan Railways lines in London. This locomotive was built in 1892 and was withdrawn in 1938. The adverts on the building are also of interest. *John Ryan Collection*

A view of Hooton station looking towards Birkenhead around 1912; note the gas lamp and ornate wooden benches. The freight train on the up fast line contains many Midland Railway open wagons. When the line was quadrupled at the turn of the last century the new lines were added on the west side of the line i.e. the former slow lines or the current lines.
John Ryan Collection

GWR 0-4-2T No. 3571 departs Hooton with local passenger train for Birkenhead in 1930. The locomotive was designed by William Dean, built at Stafford Road Works, Wolverhampton in 1895 and withdrawn in October 1942. The livery of the coaches is not the usual GWR chocolate and cream but dates between 1912 and 1922 when crimson lake livery was applied. The large factory behind belonged to Tragasol Products, who were glue (vegetable gum) manufacturers.
J.A.Peden/IRS

Two ex-Midland Railway horse boxes are alongside the loading dock in this 1930s view north of Hooton looking towards Birkenhead, with a GWR steam railmotor and trailer on the next track which served the West Kirby branch. Although generally traffic on the branch was of a local nature, from 1923 -1939 the LMS ran through carriages from New Brighton which were attached at Hooton to Birkenhead Woodside - Euston services. *J.A.Peden/IRS*

LMS 'Crab' 2-6-0 No. 42923 of Birkenhead shed, approaches Hooton station on 28th May 1962 with a short passenger train for Chester on a summer evening. It has just passed the 90 lever L&NWR Hooton North signal box, which closed on 9th December 1973. The lines in the foreground are the West Kirby lines. *J.F.Ward/ Jon Penn Collection*

LMS 'Black Five' 4-6-0 No. 45232 shunts the North Yard at Hooton in the 1960s, probably in 1967 when the locomotive was allocated to Birkenhead. This was the yard to the west side of the line opposite the North signal box. Note the rack for tail lamps outside the wooden 'Bothy'. The chimney in the background is at a former brickworks; the area now used as a landfill site. *Edgar Richards/Jon Penn Collection*

Locomotive No. 47116 unusually moves to the 'wrong line' at the north end of Hooton station on 18th May 1988 with 6E36, the 20.00 Van den Berghs to Purfleet empty oil wagons. This train ran inconveniently late on a Sunday evening and could only be photographed effectively in high summer. The site of the North Yard seen in the previous photograph is on the left. *David Pool*

In the late 1960s a green liveried Class '40' leaves the run-around loop on the former fast lines (closed in 1973) to the north of Hooton station. It is heading south towards Chester with an oil tank train from Ellesmere Port, complete with brake vans and barrier wagons. The train headcode indicates it is bound for the Birmingham Division.
Edgar Richards/Jon Penn Collection

Network Rail's DR No. 98901 leads a Rail Head Treatment Train south through Eastham Rake station on 3rd October 2018 with the 04.15 Wigan circular working, taking in all the Wirral lines of Merseyrail. Close examination of the photograph shows the high pressure water spray being applied to the top of the rail to remove debris and improve adhesion. These trains ran in the autumn, the leaf-fall season. Eastham Rake was the latest station to open, on 7th June 1995. It is popular with over a third of a million passengers normally using the station.
Chris Coxon

BROMBOROUGH

Bromborough signal box was located in the '10 foot' between the pairs of fast and slow lines and contained a 36 lever L&NWR tumbler frame; the box closed in 1985. The projections either side to assist the signalman in looking along each track, were a common feature of the signal boxes on this line.

Harry Leadbetter

A GWR 'Grange' 4-6-0 hauls a long freight train tender first through Bromborough in the 1950s. Birkenhead had an allocation of four Granges during that decade so the class was quite common on the line. A permanent way (track) gang are working on the adjacent up slow line, while coal wagons are being unloaded in the goods yard, now a car park. The signal box is just visible in the upper left of the picture.

Jon Penn Collection

A passenger train arrives on the down slow line behind a tank engine in the 1950s. The covered footbridge at the Chester end of Bromborough station is seen with associated smoke stains from departing locomotives. Also noteworthy are the tall co-acting signals at the end of the platforms, the upper arm being visible at a distance and the lower arm more easily seen closer to.

Edgar Richards/Jon Penn Collection

A GWR steam railmotor 50 is seen at Bromborough station. It is on the up fast line and the view is looking towards Chester. These units were introduced by G. J. Churchward between 1903 and 1908, with 99 trailing carriage units and 112 powered units. The train is in the crimson lake livery, dating the photograph later than 1912.
John Ryan Collection

Bromborough station is seen looking towards Birkenhead around 1907. The tracks in the foreground are the slow lines whilst the train is standing on the down fast line. A single passenger sits under the canopy, both it and the building remain to this day. Bromborough station, like Capenhurst, was built on land donated to the railway by local landowners.
John Ryan Collection

'Stanier' 2-6-4T No. 42569 passes through Bromborough on the down fast line in the early 1960s with a train for Birkenhead. This locomotive was allocated to Wigan (Central) at this time but its cleanliness is noteworthy so perhaps has been recently outshopped by Crewe Works and used by Chester depot on this express.
Edgar Richards/Jon Penn Collection

Heading northwards through Bromborough station is an unidentified Class '9F', possibly No. 92047, with a mixed freight train on the down fast line. This locomotive spent all but the first 6 months of its life on the Wirral, either at Bidston or Birkenhead. This and the adjacent platform show considerable signs of vegetation growth and lack of maintenance. The section of lighter paving slabs on the island platform show the site of the demolished waiting room building, visible in the earlier pictures.
Brian Taylor

Bromborough Rake station opened at the same time as the electrification of the line from Rock Ferry to Hooton in 1985 and was located to serve adjacent housing. On the right hand side of the photograph the expanse of greenery is the location of the former fast lines. Leading the train was No. 507002 in livery advertising Liverpool Hope University, with No. 508125 at the rear, on the southbound section of the 13.58 Chester circular service on 7th August 2020.
John Cowlishaw

SPITAL

GWR 'Prairie' Tank No. 5103 passes Spital signal box on the up slow line with a train for Chester in May 1958. The locomotive was allocated to Chester (West) shed in 1949 but was transferred to Pontypool Road very shortly after the photograph was taken. This was part of a general, but drawn out move of Western locomotives away from the area following the takeover of Birkenhead shed by the London Midland Region in April 1953. *J.A.Peden/IRS*

Spital station is seen looking towards Chester in the 1950s, showing the covered footbridge with the booking office to the left. The signal box, visible beyond the footbridge, closed on 25th June 1972 *H.B.Priestly/Pacer Archives*

A recently installed wooden waiting shelter on the island platform at Spital in the 1970s. The turnout to the former goods yard can be seen heading right into the grass under the bridge.
Lens of Sutton

A refurbished Class '101' DMU calls at Spital with a Rock Ferry to Chester service in the 1980s. In 1863 only nine trains ran in each direction a day, markedly different to today's six trains an hour. The absence of the signal box through the bridge is now apparent. The land occupied by the former fast lines was starting to become overgrown at this time.
David Southern Collection

PORT SUNLIGHT

Port Sunlight Sidings signal box opened in 1901 and controlled access to the Lever Brothers' soap works and the line to Bromborough Dock. It contained a 50 lever L&NWR tumbler frame and continued in use until 2nd November 1986. In 1985 the concrete troughing is being laid out ready for resignalling work, while the covered walkway behind connected two parts of the soap works at that time.
David Southern

A GWR '517' Class 0-4-2T passing Port Sunlight whilst working a Birkenhead Woodside to West Kirby service comprising a passenger brake and three non-corridor clerestory coaches in 1926. In the background a GWR pannier tank is visible shunting the interchange sidings. The Lever Brothers' factory visible in the background had expanded enormously during this time with very large amounts of goods being handled by the railway.
Authors' Collection

Overnight freight trains ran between the margarine works of Van den Berghs at Bromborough and Purfleet in Essex. Type TEA heated tanks were used to convey the edible soya bean oil from Essex, the usual motive power being a Class '47'. Returning empty tanks to Purfleet is No. 47203, leaving Bromborough at 20.00 as 6E36 on 5th May 1988. The train has reversed behind the Lubrizol plant, will then pass under Stadium Road and under the A41 before running round again at Port Sunlight station. Bromborough Dock was heavily used during World War 2 whilst Liverpool and Birkenhead Docks were disrupted due to bombing, with an American 0-6-0T used for shunting. This private line was used to transport coal to Bromborough Power Station from 1951, until its conversion to oil in 1958. The branch was last used in late 1992 after the expensive but short lived six year revival.

David Pool

India, a 0-6-0T built by Andrew Barclay in 1919 as their Works No. 1616, is seen shunting the exchange sidings at Port Sunlight on 16th December 1957. The locomotive saw forty years of service with Lever Bros before being scrapped in September 1959. For many years Port Sunlight produced much business for the railway with traffic increasing ten-fold in the first two decades of the twentieth century, an important factor in the quadrification of the line to Ledsham.
J.A.Peden/IRS

Port Sunlight Works operated both steam and diesel shunting locomotives and *Lord Leverhulme* is seen at Port Sunlight near the junction with the main lines. The locomotive was a 204hp 0-4-0DM built by Andrew Barclay (Works No. 388) which arrived new at the factory on 18th September 1953 as replacement for *Lifebuoy* and *Princess Mary*. Named at the factory along with No. 389 *Lady Leverhulme*, *Lord Leverhulme* was sold to Carlton Street Metals and then resold to Steamtown at Carnforth in October 1984.
David Southern

Andrew Barclay 0-4-0 saddle tank in the yard at Port Sunlight with a group of shunters. The locomotive was built in 1910 and carries the name of the then new king *King George V*. Perhaps the photograph being taken when the locomotive was new.

John Ryan Collection

A view of Port Sunlight Soap Works taken from the adjacent village about 1906. The tracks visible in the lower right of the picture were part of a 2-foot gauge tramway used to transport material arising from the works excavations to nearby marshy ground to raise ground levels. The works were established in 1888 and named after Lever Brothers' most popular product.

John Ryan Collection

BR Standard Class '9F' No. 92023, ex-Crosti boilered, hauls the evening parcel train from Woodside away from Port Sunlight station in the mid-1960s. The signal box and the junction with the Bromborough Dock branch can be seen in the background along with the exchange sidings. This train had lengthy stops at the station in order to load the many parcels from Lever Brothers and its occupation of the up fast line required express goods services to travel over the slow lines to overtake. The near platform remains to serve Liverpool bound trains. Southbound services now use a new platform built in 1968 on the land occupied by the down fast line, closed between Hooton and Rock Ferry on 21st July 1968. The new platform enabled the closure of the up fast to passenger traffic on 15th December 1968 and its continuing use as the Up Goods Line, before being taken out of use on Christmas Eve 1973.

Roger Jermy

A Stanier 2-6-4T passes through Port Sunlight on the down fast line with an express train for Birkenhead. Unlike other stations on the line Port Sunlight did not have an island platform which meant stopping trains had to be routed on the up fast line. The station was opened by King George V in 1914 exclusively for Lever Bros employees on production of a special pass. The station was enlarged with a subway in 1920 and in 1927 the general public were allowed to use the station, with ownership transferred to the railway five years later. *Edgar Richards/Jon Penn Collection*

The Bank Holiday weekend of 30th April - 2nd May 1988 saw Lever Bros. holding a Vintage Transport Weekend to mark the centenary of the works. As part of the celebrations a steam hauled passenger service operated from Port Sunlight to Bromborough Dock. Ex-GWR 'Small Prairie' No. 4566 from the Severn Valley Railway is at the temporary platform erected at Port Sunlight station for this service. *David Southern*

LMS 'Crab' No. 42727 2-6-0 enters Port Sunlight station with the evening parcels working from Woodside to Chester consisting of two Southern Railway CCT vans and an LMS 6 wheeler wagon, likely to be in the period March 1966 to April 1967 when it was allocated to Birkenhead. This locomotive was somewhat a 'pet' engine of the shed and was well kept by enthusiasts, for use on railtours. *Edgar Richards/Jon Penn Collection*

With the boiler pressure nicely on the limit Aston shed's clean LMS 'Stanier' Black 5 No. 44872 heads south on the up slow line at Port Sunlight on 13th July 1962, with the 7.15 pm Morpeth Docks to Aston Goods fitted van freight. This train was probably routed over the slow line to pass the parcels train seen in the photograph above.
Edgar Richards/Jon Penn Collection

A Class '56' hauls a coal train south through Port Sunlight during an eight month period of importation from Bidston Dock to Fiddlers Ferry Power Station in 1986.
Edgar Richards/Jon Penn Collection

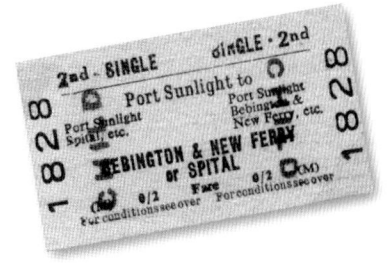

Bebington & New Ferry station is seen in the 1960s looking north towards Rock Ferry showing the tall signals at the platform ends. The signal box located centrally between the pairs of lines contained a 36 lever L&NWR tumbler frame and was closed on 18th September 1974. Note the water treatment tank in the goods yard, which supplied softened water to Birkenhead shed. Two ex-L&NWR tenders, still lettered LMS, survived here until the 1960s in use as sludge carriers for the treatment plant. *H.B.Priestly/Pacer Archives*

A very clean L&NWR 'Super D' with an Edge Hill shed plate enters Bebington & New Ferry station with a freight train in May 1958, watched by a ganger standing by his Permanent Way hut. The suffix '& New Ferry' was dropped from the station name in 1974. *Authors' collection*

On 5th March 1967 two trains (A & B), 'Farewell to the G.W.R. Birmingham - Birkenhead Service', were organised by the Stephenson Locomotive Society (Midland Area) from Birmingham Snow Hill to commemorate the end of express services from Birkenhead. Class '9F' No. 92234 heads northwards through Bebington & New Ferry station on the down slow line with the third component of 'Train A's schedule, 13.30 Chester - Woodside. *David Pool*

ROCK FERRY

'Stanier' 2-6-4T No. 42611 collects empty coal wagons from Rock Ferry goods yard, just south of the station, possibly between July 1965 and July 1966 when it was allocated to Springs Branch depot in Wigan. Meanwhile wagons on an adjacent line are being unloaded onto a coal lorry. The booking office with its lantern style roof can be seen on the road overbridge To the south of this location the original station of Rock Lane was located; this closed in 1862 as the commercial centre had moved north to the south side of Bedford Road as seen in the background. Until 1887 the station was located in this area until the coming of the Mersey Railway demanded greater space which was provided on the north side of Bedford Road. *Edgar Richards/Jon Penn Collection*

The booking office at Rock Ferry although not a standard L&NWR design had many similar features to other stations on the joint line, as seen in the photograph from the 1950s. These buildings were demolished and a more basic booking office provided at low level to the left, in front of the bay platforms.

Edgar Richards/Jon Penn Collection

A Whale L&NWR 'Renown' Class 4-4-0 departs Rock Ferry for Chester with a train of L&NWR coaches in the early 1920s. The locomotives were built in Crewe between 1897 and 1903 and were withdrawn in the period 1925-1931. This section of line south of the station towards Bebington is the most extensive cutting on the line, the spoil from which was used for the embankment north of the station and also south of Bebington.

E.C. Lloyd Collection

An identical view to the previous one but this time showing a GWR '43XX' Class 'Mogul' with a train of GWR coaches, on a Chester bound train at the south end of Rock Ferry station. These two photographs encapsulate the joint line passenger services at this period with both companies providing motive power and stock.

E.C. Lloyd Collection

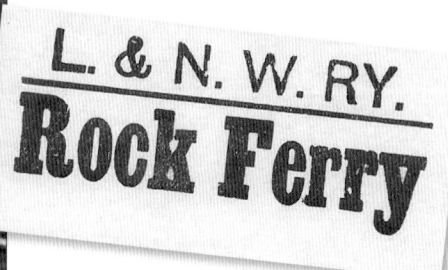

Class '24' No. 5043 passes through Rock Ferry on the down goods (former fast) line with a freight train for Birkenhead Docks around 1970. The DMUs on the right working services towards Chester. By this time the original station buildings seen earlier on the bridge had been demolished. *Pacer Archives*

A two-car DMU stands in the Chester platform at Rock Ferry whilst working a special charter train for the Wirral Railway Circle. In the electrified bay platform 3 on the right, a Class '503' EMU waits to depart for Liverpool. *Edgar Richards/Jon Penn Collection*

After the closure of Birkenhead Woodside station in 1967 the slow lines were severed and converted into the two bay platforms for services to Chester as seen in the foreground in December 1968. A Class '503' passes the signal box towards the original Mersey Railway bay platforms with a terminating service from Liverpool.

Pacer Archives

A Class '47' is the subject of railway enthusiasts' cameras as it approaches Rock Ferry from Birkenhead on the then singled up & down goods line on 13th April 1985. In the foreground, work is in progress for the reconnection of the slow lines to the electrified lines as part of the Rock Ferry - Hooton electrification scheme. The buffers and walkway across the Chester bay platforms have been removed by this time.

David Southern

The northern end of Rock Ferry Station looking towards Birkenhead taken in March 1956, showing the period when two signal boxes were present during rebuilding. The flat roofed box nearer the platforms was the BR replacement for the older L&NWR box, originally known as Mersey Junction, in the background. The BR box was commissioned the following year with a 60 lever LM standard frame. While the signals at the platform end are all of the modern upper quadrant type there are still a few L&NWR lower quadrant signals in the distance near the old box. The signals on the left are cleared for an electric service heading to Liverpool and on the right for a train to move from the fast lines over to the slow lines using the crossover beyond the platform. *J.A.Peden/IRS*

The facing crossover between the slow lines and the electrified lines to the left had been removed since the previous photograph and so the left hand posts of both signals have lost their arms. An unidentified BR '9F' 2-10-0 approaches Rock Ferry with a cattle train from Birkenhead in the 1960s on the up slow line. *Edgar Richards/Jon Penn Collection*

Looking north from Rock Ferry station showing Birkenhead allocated 'Stanier' 4MT 2-6-4T No. 42658 arriving into the station with a stopping passenger train on the up fast line on a sunny 25th May 1962, four months before withdrawal. The train has just moved to the right to enter the platform, a result of the widening of the formation to accommodate the double track extension of the Mersey Railway into Rock Ferry around 1890. The Joint Railway constructed additional tracks to the east here and recovered its costs from the then moribund Mersey Railway by taking a share of future revenues. *Edgar Richards/Jon Penn Collection*

On 14th August 1902 a Webb L&NWR Special 'DX' Class 0-6-0 No. 1355 leaves Rock Ferry for Birkenhead Woodside under the watchful eye of a track worker. The first vehicle behind the locomotive is an L&NWR Horsebox, while the coaches are GWR. The locomotive class, originally totalling 943 examples, were long lasting with the final one being withdrawn in 1930. Although primarily goods engines they were vacuum brake fitted upon rebuilding and so able to work passenger trains. *LCGB/Ken Nunn Collection*

The luggage lifts are a prominent feature in this view of a 'Fairburn' 2-6-4T about to depart Rock Ferry for Birkenhead Woodside in the 1950s.
Edgar Richards/Jon Penn Collection

BR 'Standard' Class No. 73141, with Caprotti valve gear is the subject of another enthusiast's camera at Rock Ferry. The locomotive along with the other Caprotti valve gear fitted engines were transferred to Patricroft shed in Manchester in 1964 and so the photograph is presumed to date between June 1964 and the locomotives withdrawal in July 1967. At that time smokebox number and shed code plates were being removed or stolen and this locomotive is fitted with amateurish replacements.
Brian Taylor

Viewed from the signal box, a Fairburn 2-6-4T leaves Rock Ferry for Birkenhead Woodside with through carriages from London Paddington in the 1950s. The luggage lifts are dominant together with the backs of the terraced houses of Lees Avenue adjacent to the line.
Edgar Richards/Jon Penn Collection

Looking south towards Rock Ferry from Green Lane Junction signal box on 18th January 1986 as two Class '33's, No. 33051 and No. 33062, haul the 'Wirral Widdershins' railtour from London Victoria, which traversed the MDHB lines returning via Wrexham. The open land previously occupied by the fast lines is apparent in this view, latterly occupied by the up through siding to Rock Ferry taken out of use on 27th February 1973. *David Southern*

With the signalman posing proudly at the top of the steps of the original L&NWR signal box at Green Lane Junction; a view looking towards Rock Ferry in the 1920s with the exit from Green Lane Goods Yard in the foreground and headshunt. The coal bunker is visible in the left foreground and the fogman's hut next to the steps. *Glyn Parry Collection*

The replacement Green Lane Junction signal box was opened by the LMS in 1931 with a 60 lever tappet frame. The box was starting to look a little dilapidated when this view was taken in the 1980s; it finally closed on 3rd December 1986. New Chester Road at a lower level is behind the signal box. In front of the retaining wall in the foreground are the Mersey Railway electrified lines descending into Green Lane station. *David Southern*

Having just passed the bridge over Chamberlain Street on 26th September 1958 LMS Stanier 2-6-0 42977 on an up stopping train is signalled to cross over from the fast to the slow lines, whilst GWR 'Mogul' No. 6346 waits to leave Green Lane Sidings with a train of empty mineral wagons for collieries in the Wrexham area. Just visible through the smoke on the extreme right is a pannier tank with brake vans at the beginning of Green Lane High Level Sidings.
J.A.Peden/IRS

Looking north from Green Lane Junction signal box on 18th January 1986 as the 'Wirral Widdershins' railtour from London Victoria heads towards the MDHB lines. This contrasts with the previous picture as the eight lines were by then reduced to two. In former days the Mollington Street depot and Blackpool Street signal box, 529 yards away, would be visible in this view. The land in the foreground showing evidence that the last remnants of Green Lane Sidings had been lifted by this date.
David Southern

A GWR 'Metro' 2-4-0T passes the impressive signal gantry at Green Lane Junction in the 1920s, heading towards Birkenhead Woodside on a short train of L&NWR coaches. As at Hooton, rings were the L&NWR's method of showing which signals applied to the goods line, these were discontinued from 1926.
Glyn Parry Collection

A slightly more distant view of Green Lane Junction shows a GWR '43XX' Class 'Mogul' heading for Birkenhead Woodside with an express on the fast line comprised of GWR stock around 1925.
Glyn Parry Collection

In the late 1950s LMS 'Stanier' 2-6-4T No. 42447 passes Blackpool Street carriage sidings with the stock of the through train to Deal in Kent, the first five coaches being of Southern stock. The locomotive was allocated to Birkenhead between August 1956 and June 1961. A GWR pannier tank is again the yard shunter in Green Lane Sidings and the coaling plant of Mollington Street shed is visible behind the first coach, with the gas works beyond.
Edgar Richards/Jon Penn Collection

In July 1958 GWR 2-6-2T No. 4115 passes Green Lane Junction on a down train of LMS coaches. The locomotive was transferred away from Chester (West) shed the following month to Newton Abbot in Devon. Cammell Laird's shipyard is in the background. *J.A.Peden/IRS*

BIRKENHEAD MOLLINGTON STREET MOTIVE POWER DEPOT

Mollington Street shed was opened jointly by the L&NWR and the GWR in 1878 and finally closed to steam in November 1967. It was a large 16 road shed with the two companies having 8 roads each. Both sections had a 'Northlight' pattern roof, the L&NWR section being replaced in 1938 with a longitudinal multi-pitched roof and was curtailed in length. Each company originally had a turntable on its own side of the shed before a new larger one was built in the 1930s near the shed entrance.

In the mid-1950s a new mechanical coal and two ash plants were added along with a servicing shed for diesel shunters. After the end of steam the shed continued in use as a diesel depot, and in its final years was used for the storage and stripping of the Merseyrail Class '503' EMUs before finally closing on the 25th November 1985. The shed was demolished in July 1987.

In 1958 there were 260 men employed there of which 100 were drivers, 100 firemen, 12 fitting staff, 10 cleaners and 8 clerical staff, with the remainder labourers and general staff. The shed had a 70 foot diameter turntable large enough to turn a 9F. The last steam locomotive to be turned at Mollington Street was '9F' No. 92203 which worked the final steam hauled iron ore train from Bidston Dock to Shotton Steelworks, on 6th November 1967. The practice was to use the turntable so that every locomotive leaving the shed faced in a southerly direction. Earlier that year on 5th March 1967, the shed had provided two Stanier tanks to haul the last Paddington train between Birkenhead Woodside and Chester. Under the Great Western Railway the shed was coded BHD; the joint shed becoming 6C under British Railways until September 1963 when it changed to 8H. Under the TOPS system it was coded BC.

Taken from the coaling plant looking towards the shed entrance on 3rd April 1958 a 'Crab' Class locomotive is entering Hinderton Field Coal Yard loaded with domestic coal; the yard closed in 1970. The other locomotives visible are a GWR pannier tank and an LMS 0-4-0 saddle tank, possibly on locomotive coal. In the background behind the signal gantry is Green Lane signal box and to the left of the 'Crab' its signal controlling the exit. Hidden in the steam are Green Lane End sidings.
J.A.Peden/IRS

Stanier '8F' No. 48476 cautiously negotiates the pointwork as it enters the shed yard over Green Lane bridge in 1965. This location was popular with local train spotters in the 1950s and 1960s.
Pacer Archives

GWR *Dean* 517 'Open Cab' Class 0-4-2T No. 3579 at the shed entrance. The locomotive entered service in December 1895 and was withdrawn in July 1942. *F.A.G.H.Coltas*

LMS '3F' 0-6-0T *Jinty* No. 47674 is standing on the entrance tracks to Mollington Street shed, carrying the reporting number 0Z80 denoting its participation in a railtour. The locomotive spent all its life on the Wirral, either at Bidston or Mollington Street; it was withdrawn in December 1966. *Pacer Archives*

Also at the shed entrance with Blackpool Street Carriage Sidings and Green Lane Goods Yard behind, is an even more ancient North London Railway dock tank, No. 58857, built 8 years before in 1887. However this locomotive lasted longer than the GWR tank when it was withdrawn from Bow Road in London in 1958. The date of the photograph is 10th June 1950 which is between its BR numbering in January 1950 and its transfer south in November 1952.
Edgar Richards/Jon Penn Collection

A number of locomotives cluster around the coal and ash plants including '9F' No. 92123, a 'Crab' No. 42782 and an '8F' in the mid-1960s. Immediately behind the coaling plant the tunnel of the Mersey Railway is located on its way to Birkenhead Central station. *Norman E. Preedy / Kidderminster Museum*

The new coal and ash plants are seen under construction at Birkenhead shed in May 1955. In the foreground is the Great Western standard coaling stage, with water tank above, having replaced the original coaling stage. An air raid shelter entrance is seen in the centre of the photograph.
J.A.Peden/IRS

In 1961 The GWR (right) section of the shed was curtailed in length and re-roofed to match the previously re-roofed L&NWR section, as seen from the top of the coaling plant. The wall on the extreme right hand side shows the original length of both parts of the shed. The shed on the extreme left was built for diesel shunters in the mid-1950s with the loss of four roads of the L&NWR shed. Several diesel locomotives can be seen although heavily outnumbered by steam and in the foreground are the two ash disposal plants. *Brian Elliot Collection*

An Armstrong GWR 2-4-0 locomotive is seen alongside the original GWR coal stage at Birkenhead, shortly after opening in 1879.
C. Heywood/Jon Penn Collection

Class '03' No. 03189 and a Class '47' keep company with a tunnel inspection coach inside the diesel shunter extension of Mollington Street depot in the 1970s.
David Southern

Locomotives visible in this mid-1950s view of Mollington Street depot include GWR 0-4-'2T' No. 1457, two '41XX' 2-6-2 tanks, a 'WD' 2-8-0 and a GW '28XX' 2-8-0 No. 2822.
ccH.C. Casserley

Dating probably during the early 1950s a group of shed staff pose alongside GWR 2-6-2T No. 4129, retaining its GWR lettering on the side tanks but having been fitted with a BR smoke box number plate. The locomotive was at Birkenhead at nationalisation and left for Cardiff Cathays in 1957. The shorter length and the different roof of the former L&NWR section of the shed is noticeable in this photograph, with the longer GWR side wall and its original 'Northlight' roof visible on the right.
Authors' Collection

Locomotives visible in this early-1950s view of the L&NWR side of Mollington Street depot include ex-L&YR Aspinall 0-6-0 No. 52225, a L&NWR Bowen-Cooke 'G2' Class 0-8-0 and two LMS Stanier Prairie tanks.
Authors' Collection

A Stanier '8F' 2-8-0 is seen amongst the grime and dust of the coaling plant in the summer of 1967. *David Southern*

GWR 'Grange' Class 4-6-0 No. 6851 *Hurst Grange* is caught in the sunlight outside the shed in this 1960s photograph. *Pacer Archives*

On the left of this view of Mollington Street depot in the mid-1980s a LMS designed Class '503' unit is awaiting removal for scrapping alongside its replacement No. 508020 which waits to enter service. The large gas holders are now a thing of the past with the demise of town gas. By this date the number of lines to the shed had been severely reduced, with only the L&NWR section remaining. *David Southern*

This 1960s view really captures the oil and grime of a working steam shed. The locomotives are GWR 2-8-0 No. 3812 and Crewe based LMS Class '5' 4-6-0 No. 44832. The gallows like structure above 3812 was to indicate to firemen the maximum height they could raise fire irons when working under overhead electric wires.
Norman Kneale

Class '8F' 2-8-0 No. 48319 in front of one of the ash plants in the mid-1960s. *David Southern*

Looking towards two ash plants are two Class '8F's, examples of this once numerous class in Birkenhead. *C.P. Stacey*

This panorama was taken from the coaling plant of Mollington Street shed with the 70 foot turntable installed in the late 1930s in the foreground. The gasworks can be seen on the left, while coke wagons are present in the sidings behind the two Blackpool Street signal boxes. Blackpool Street Carriage Sidings, developed in the 1880s are beyond, with the curved Abbey Street sidings in the distance and part of Cammell Laird shipyard visible in the background. The Liver Building is on the skyline. *C. Heywood/Jon Penn Collection*

Class '9F' No. 92069 is having trouble using the turntable as the driver is trying to repair the vacuum pipe from the locomotive to the turntable's motor seemingly ineffectively as a large number of young railwaymen are struggling to turn the 140 ton engine. The locomotive was allocated to Birkenhead between 1965 and 1967. Behind are the two signal boxes at Blackpool Street and to the left the gasworks. *Pacer Archives*

BLACKPOOL STREET

On 27th May 1958 LMS 'Stanier' 2-6-4T No. 42493 with an up train of GWR non-corridor stock passes a down working at Blackpool Street. The locomotive was a long term resident of Birkenhead, allocated there from December 1956 until withdrawal in May 1964. Green Lane High Level Sidings are on the right.
J.A.Peden/IRS

A grimy LMS Stanier '8F' 2-8-0 passes Blackpool Street with an up cattle train from Morpeth Dock in Birkenhead, late on a summer evening in the 1960s. At this time these 8Fs were common at Birkenhead with 31 based there in February 1965 but by the June they had all been transferred away. The down line towards Woodside station has been signalled as a clear road.
Edgar Richards/Jon Penn Collection

Class '25' No. D7558 is seen at Blackpool Street on the up goods line from Birkenhead Docks. The signal near the locomotive which applied to the down fast line has lost its arms indicating the photograph dates from after the closure of Woodside station and Blackpool Street signal box in November 1967. Blackpool Street Sidings on the right, access to which was controlled from Green Lane Junction, are being used to stable DMUs and coal wagons.
Pacer Archives

The lines to the left lead to the dock extension goods lines, passing through the four-track Haymarket Tunnel, and those on the right lead to Birkenhead Town and Woodside stations. In the centre of the picture between these sets of lines is the site of Grange Lane, the original terminus of the line from Chester. The vans on the extreme right hand side are on Blackpool Street sidings. BR Standard Class '4' 2-6-0 No. 75054 is on an up express and is seen passing Blackpool Street signal box, an elevated L&NWR structure spanning a track. Adjacent is a British Railways box built as a replacement in the early 1960s but never brought into service, as in 1966 the box was dismantled and re-erected at Coton Hill South at Shrewsbury, where the previous box had been destroyed by a runaway accident on 11th January 1965. A section of the frame was not needed at Coton Hill and was used in Birkenhead Park Signal Box. The original box closed on 5th November 1967 when the line to Woodside closed and this location ceased to be a junction.
Brian Taylor

In May 1958 Stanier 'Mogul' No. 42970 leaves Blackpool Street Carriage Sidings with the stock for the Birkenhead to London Euston train as indicated by the nameboard on the carriage. An LMS 2-6-4 tank and a GWR pannier tank are visible on the right. Stanier 'Mogul's were common on the Wirral with half of the class being allocated to Birkenhead at some stage. On the left hand side of the picture, the Gas Works and associated gantries are visible. From the closure of Woodside to express trains on 5th March 1967 the carriage sidings turned over to wagon storage, until closure in December 1970.

Authors' Collection

A rebuilt L&NWR 'Precursor' Class 4-4-0 is seen passing Birkenhead Town Station tender first on its way back to Mollington Street shed from Woodside station in the early 1930s. Blackpool Street Carriage Sidings and the carriage shed are in the background. The 1 in 95 gradient rising towards Green Lane is evident in this photograph, when compared to the more level sidings. *Glyn Parry Collection*

An exterior view of the then Birkenhead Town station complete with tarpaulin covered lorry in the 1960s. It is of similar architectural style to Rock Ferry and the station was located close to the original Grange Lane terminus. The station was built in 1889 after complaints from the local residents that there was no station between Woodside and Rock Ferry, a distance of around 2 miles. *Authors' Collection*

Stanier 'Mogul' No. 42977 passing through the derelict Birkenhead Town Station with an up express on 26th September 1958. Despite having been closed since 1945 the buildings are in reasonable condition, though the platform edge copers have been partly removed. The train emerges from the 565 yard long tunnel from Woodside under Chester Road and was working hard up the steep 1 in 95 gradient. Immediately to the right of this tunnel and behind the tall brick wall was an adjoining tunnel leading to the second terminus at Monk's Ferry, closed in 1967. At the end of the platform is Blackpool Street's starting signal with Woodside's fixed distant underneath along with a subsidiary signal. *J.A.Peden/IRS*

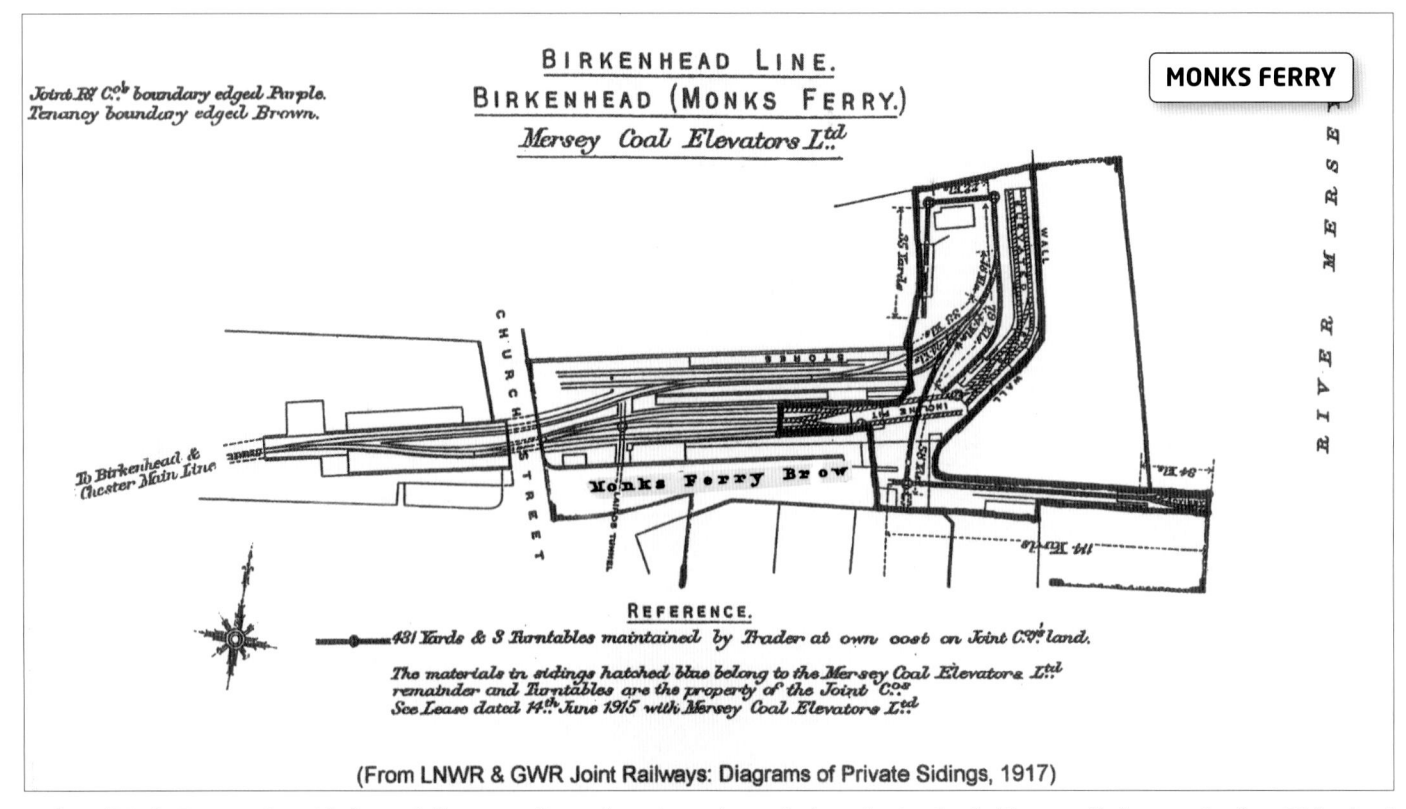

(From LNWR & GWR Joint Railways: Diagrams of Private Sidings, 1917)

A plan of Monks Ferry station with the goods lines extending and turning to the north along the river bank. The tunnelled connection from Birkenhead Town is shown on the left with the tunnel access to Cammell Laird's heading south, to the east of Church Street. This fell into disuse in 1908, with the yard served from Green Lane Sidings.

Monks Ferry on 16th March 1948 looking towards the 436 yard long single line tunnel from Birkenhead Town Station, with a number of mineral wagons on the right and railway offices on the left. The station was opened on 23rd October 1844 by Sir Philip Egerton, the same day as the foundations were laid for Birkenhead Docks. It was here that the first through train to London Paddington ran after completion of the 'narrow gauge' lines in 1861. Until 1878 when Woodside station opened, it was the main terminus in Birkenhead. *C.H.A.Townley/J.A.Peden Collection/IRS*

A three-tub coal wagon No. 74 in Monks Ferry Yard on 4th November 1958. The small tubs were emptied by crane directly into the bunkers of steam powered tugs and this system continued until the steam tugs were replaced by diesel powered vessels. The arched wall behind the wagon once supported a train shed over the passenger platforms. *J.A.Peden/IRS*

Three-tub wagons at Monks Ferry on 29th April 1958; the right hand tub on both wagons carries a plate 'Ifton', being the colliery in North Shropshire that supplied the coal. The yard closed in 1961 as by then most ships were oil powered but the tracks were not lifted until 1967.   *J.A.Peden/IRS*

A train conveying coal tubs is seen entering Monks Ferry Yard in the 1950s behind the Kitson 0-4-0T *Lively Polly* formerly owned by the Liverpool Overhead Railway. Monks Ferry was converted into a coal handling wharf in 1878 when it closed as a passenger terminus following the opening of Woodside station. An overall roof was present until at least 1948 between the arched wall and the retaining wall on the right hand side.
Turner/Birkenhead Libraries

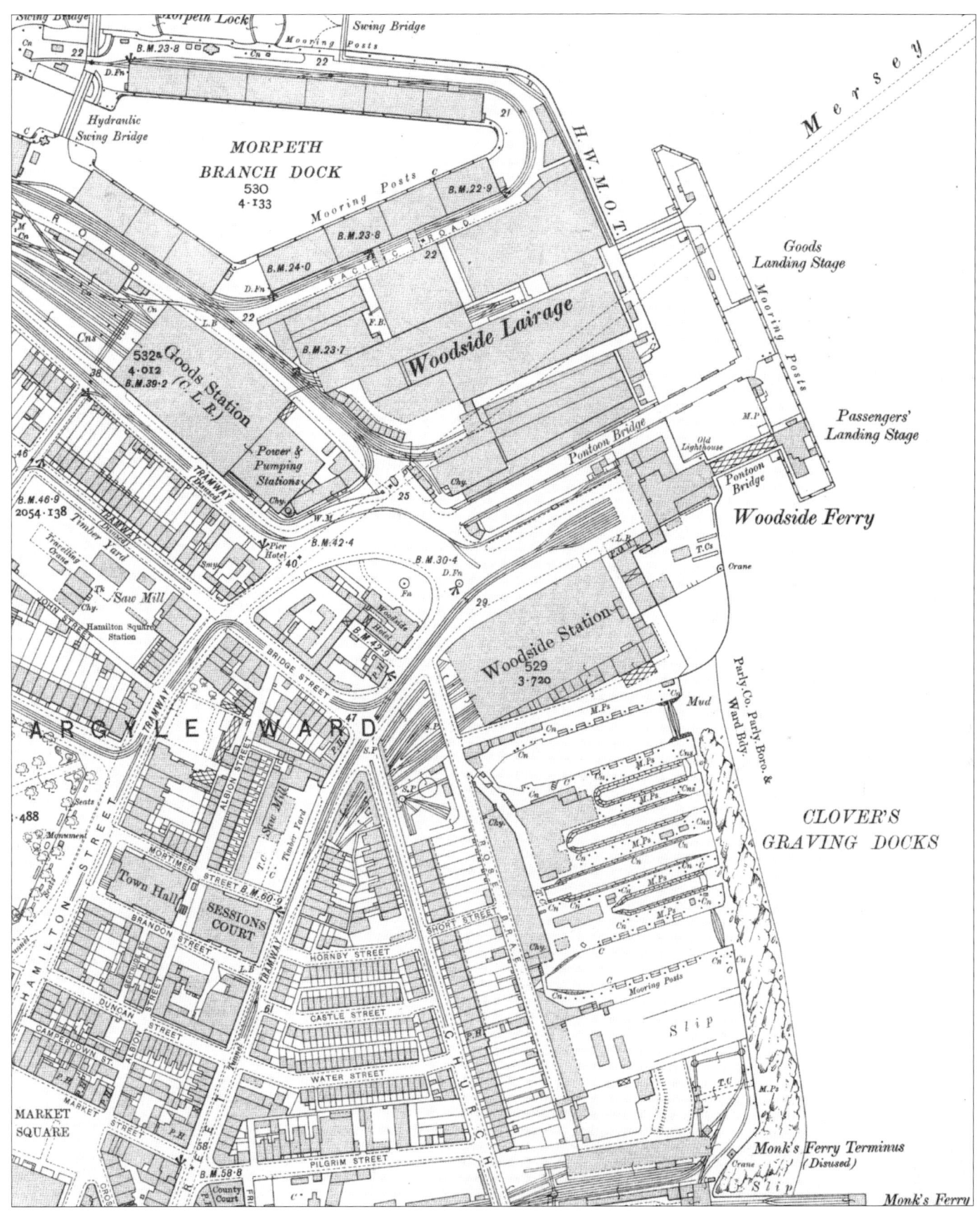

An extract of the 1911 Ordnance Survey map showing Woodside station, with the original layout of the turntable and servicing facility on the south side of the station. Woodside was to provide a fully serviced station as the facilities at Monks Ferry were deemed inadequate and too far upstream of Liverpool to offer a good ferry service. A new line was built from Grange Lane of just over half a mile in length and known as the Birkenhead New Line. The majority of the line was in tunnel under Chester Road, the cut-and-cover construction being highly disruptive.
To the north of the station was the substantial Woodside Lairage for the importation of cattle, principally from Ireland.

The unusual 0-4-0T which operated at Monks Ferry was built by Kitson of Leeds in 1893 to their tram locomotive design and supplied new to the Liverpool Overhead Railway. In 1949 it was bought by Rea Ltd who operated the Monks Ferry site for the coaling of tugs and other smaller vessels. It was broken up in 1961 following closure of the yard. During its time on the LOR it was known by the staff as *Lively Polly*. *Edgar Richards/Jon Penn Collection*

BIRKENHEAD WOODSIDE

The station throat at Woodside, possibly taken from the rear of a steam hauled train. The track veering off to the right is the approach to the former engine servicing yard and turntable. It had been blocked off at the far end of the tunnel in the 1960s. This area was originally planned to be part of the tunnel but the need to enlarge the track layout made this impractical, and the tunnel curtailed. *Jon Penn Collection*

L&NWR 'George the Fifth' Class 4-4-0 No. 5365 *Racehorse* departs Woodside and enters the tunnel under Chester Road to Birkenhead Town station in the 1930s, whilst two gangers return to the platform. The first coach is a GWR 'Toplight' vehicle above which can be seen the original signal box. Note on the left hand bridge abutment the joint L&NWR/GWR bridge plate. *E.C. Lloyd Collection*

GWR 4-6-0 No. 6844 *Penhydd Grange* faces the gloomy Woodside Tunnel in the early 1950s when the locomotive was allocated to Birkenhead. The original signal box is visible above the engine and the water tank and shunters' cabin on the left are adjacent to the old turntable road. *Roger Carpenter*

A GWR '3571' Class 0-4-2T departs Woodside for Chester with a local service. This class of only 10 locomotives were designed by Armstrong at Stafford Road Works in Wolverhampton in 1895 and were generally used in this area, the last being withdrawn in 1949. *Roger Carpenter*

This photograph is the first of two taken in April 1930. GWR 'Dean' 2-4-2T No. 3627 leaves Woodside, the locomotive being built in 1903 and withdrawn from Birkenhead in 1934. These engines were nicknamed 'Birdcages' and were built for London and Birmingham suburban services before being transferred to the Wirral. The top of the hydraulic lift shaft serving Mersey Railway's Hamilton Square station is visible in the background. Note the brickwork parapet above the stone retaining wall and the very full bunker of the locomotive. *F.A.G.H.Coltas*

An L&NWR Webb 5ft 6in. 2-4-2T No. 6649 coupled to GWR coaches at Woodside. Note the two gangers by the coach and the sturdy L&NWR bracket signal.
F.A.G.H.Coltas

In this scene 'Stanier' Class 3 2-6-2T, No. 40128 is leaving platform 4 at Woodside with a local service formed of GWR coaches, while Stanier 'Mogul' No. 42969 stands in platform 5. The tank engine was allocated to Birkenhead between 1952 and 1956 with the 'Mogul' being allocated there for a very long time, between 1940 and 1962.
Authors' Collection

'Fairburn' Class 4 2-6-4T No. 42236 is waiting at platform 1 for the run to Chester with a Paddington train in the early 1960s, the shadows indicating a late afternoon departure. *Authors' Collection*

On 5th March 1967 Stanier '4P' 2-6-4T No. 42616 stands in Woodside in a clean condition no doubt because of the celebrations of the last day of through services to Paddington. The locomotive was only allocated to Birkenhead from February 1966 to May 1967.
Authors' Collection

In this 1960s view along the carriage road between platforms 1 and 2, two Ford Prefect vans and a Morris Minor can be seen with the bow of a ship dwarfing the signal box and station.
Authors' Collection

Looking towards the tunnel in the final week of Woodside on 28th October 1967, the new BR built signal box has been squeezed into the space between the railway and the graving dock to the left. Note the miniature arm L&NWR ground signal controlling the exit from the centre road and the smoke stained left hand signal arm on the bracket. The area is now used as a bus parking area for services terminating at Woodside and is quite recognisable, although the general level of the land has been raised to platform level and the houses in the background demolished.
David Southern

'Fairburn' 2-6-4T No. 42202 waits with a passenger train at Woodside, while alongside a DMU with 'speed whiskers' but no yellow warning panel is on a service to Chester. The photograph was taken in the early 1960s.
Authors' Collection

BR 'Standard' Class 4MT No. 76095 waits at the end of platform 1 for the signal to run back tender first to Mollington Street shed, in the 18 month period when it was allocated to Chester, from August 1965. With the exception of up to 49 Class '9F's allocated in mid-1965, BR 'Standard' locomotives were uncommon in Birkenhead with only a couple of '5MT' engines, some '4MT' and '2MT' tanks allocated, the last of which left in late 1961. Note Blackpool Street's up distant signal mounted on a bracket by the tunnel portal to afford clear siting before entering Woodside tunnel.
Brian Taylor

Stanier 2-6-4T No. 42616 is ready to depart with the 08.35 to Paddington on 4th March 1967, the last day of such operation, hence its very clean condition. The Woodside Hotel, seen above the parapet, was promoting the local Birkenhead Ales.
P.J.Woodhouse

Looking from the end of Platform 1 in October 1965, the longest platform face in Woodside at 537 feet, the carriage road alongside is host to a Ford Consul near the gates and a Scammell Mechanical Horse trailer in the background. Also note the platform ticket vending machine in the foreground.
Transport Treasury

In the early 1960s Fairburn 2-6-4T No. 42283 is awaiting departure at Platform 5 with the first coach of GWR Hawksworth design. Note the sharply curving platforms and check rails fitted to the track, and the gloom of the train shed caused by World War 2 damage to the glazing not being replaced.
Authors' Collection

Probably taken in the early 1950s as there are BR class markings on the LMS non-corridor coaches in platform 3, the detailed brickwork above the buffer stops can be seen along with the decorated cast iron roof columns. The large clock was made by 'Joyce, Whitchurch' at a cost of £70, a prolific manufacturer of railway clocks, whilst the light coloured structure in the distance was the booking office.
National Railway Museum

The decorative ecclesiastical style roof rafters in the original booking hall, beautifully carved but generally unseen and unadmired at a cost of just under £20,000 in 1878. The station was designed by the architect, Robert Johnson.
Stan Roberts Collection

Another scene showing the intended main entrance and booking hall with stonework detail over the windows and at the base of the roof supports. The wooden dividers and small office reflect the actual use of the area for parcels, not passengers. *Stan Roberts Collection*

A close up of one end of the 'temporary' booking office which was actually used throughout the life of the station, unlike the unused grand booking hall shown earlier.
Brian Elliot

The scene outside Birkenhead Woodside about 1910 as depicted on a commercial postcard. The railway station is on the right and the ferry terminal in the centre. This could be considered an early example of a transport interchange with railway, ferry and trams in close proximity. In later years the parcels office became public conveniences. Immediately to the left of the parcels office was the landward end of the long floating roadway which served the goods landing stage, north of Woodside ferry terminal. *John Ryan Collection*

By the 1930s the scene at Woodside is much less crowded and the trams have been abandoned in favour of buses. The buses display two liveries, the original maroon and white and the new blue and cream. The ferry terminal is advertising its services more prominently and the station proudly proclaims its joint ownership by the LMS and GWR. *Harry Leadbetter Collection*

In 1967 the mode of public transport was the motor bus and this picture taken in the evening shows clearly the excellent transport interchange available between the ferries, rail and buses at Woodside with only a small distance to the Mersey Railway station at Hamilton Square. The Catholic cathedral can be seen on the skyline nearing completion in Liverpool. The area between the ferry terminal and the former station is now occupied by a submarine museum with a U-boat.
Ward/RCTS Archive WRD00574

An evening view of Woodside station exterior in the 1950s showing the 'temporary' entrance used in place of the main entrance which was largely unknown on the south side of the station. This situation was caused by Birkenhead Corporation laying out the new tramway terminus where the bus stops can be seen in the photograph. The building in the left foreground was originally a Post Office but was then a motoring school.
National Railway Museum

This is the first of a series of photographs taken in 1957 for Grayson, Rollo and Clover Docks Ltd to record the extension of their No. 1 Graving dock, adjacent to Woodside Station into the former locomotive servicing area. The original main entrance to the station can be clearly seen with its ornate *porte-cochère*, while in the foreground are the old locomotive yard, water tank and turntable. The lane, Rose Brae, ran between the walls behind the tank and the dock. *Wirral Archives*

Although this photograph taken on 27th March 1958 was to show the erection of a concrete batching plant for the dock extension works, it also shows the buildings outside the end wall of the station and the curved train shed roofs. The elegant *porte-cochère* over the planned main entrance close to the intended ferry berth along the south side of the station can be seen. *Wirral Archives*

On 28th July 1958, the excavation work had extended landwards reaching Rose Brae, with the bridge over the station platforms closed off prior to demolition. In the foreground the turntable and rail tracks have been removed with a compressor standing by. The station alongside operates normally with LMS and GWR tanks visible and a corporation bus about to pass the Woodside Hotel. On the left hand side is the rear wall of the signal box. *Wirral Archives*

ABOVE: This early 1960s aerial view shows the complete graving dock complex operated by Grayson, Rollo and Clover Ltd. The extension to the No. 1 Dock (far right) is now complete and in use. The graving dock now extends to Church Road while Rose Brae has been removed completely. The dock has also been widened, so restricting the distance to the station buildings. The alignment of Woodside tunnel leading away under Chester Road can been determined from this photograph.
Harry Leadbetter Collection

RIGHT: The interior of the former Grange Lane locomotive shed is seen just before demolition in the 1970s. This was the original locomotive shed for the Chester & Birkenhead Railway and was in use from the 1840s until the new shed at Mollington Street opened in 1878. After this date it was used as a goods depot until the early 1920s when it was sold to a brewers' merchant; the original rails being still in situ.
Birkenhead Libraries

Chapter Two
BIRKENHEAD DOCKS EXTENSION RAILWAY

At the beginning of the 19th century Birkenhead was a small village on the Wirral peninsula with a population of just 100 whilst Liverpool on the opposite bank of the Mersey was a prosperous port with a population of 77,000. The opening of several steam ferry services between Birkenhead and Liverpool around 1820 led to an expansion of Birkenhead as many wealthy merchants chose to live there and commute across the river to Liverpool.

The expansion of Birkenhead and the severe overcrowding of the century-old docks in Liverpool, led to proposals for the construction of docks on the Wirral side of the Mersey based on the Wallasey Pool, a natural inlet at the mouth of the River Birkett, which extended some two miles inland from the river. The first proposals were put forward in 1828 due to the efforts of entrepreneur William Laird, who had also set up a shipyard on the edge of the Wallasey Pool. One of the schemes involved building a five mile long canal from the River Dee but this along with other early schemes failed due to Liverpool Council buying land to thwart competition to Liverpool docks. Nothing further happened until 1843 when new proposals were put before Parliament. These were successful and construction began in 1844 with the first two docks, Egerton and Morpeth, opening in April 1847.

These early docks were initially unsuccessful due to their poor construction and lack of accommodation, but further construction and repairs were not possible due to financial difficulties. The promised trade did not materialise and so the newly opened railways saw little income from freight traffic. This prompted the GWR to put a bill before Parliament to transfer ownership of the Liverpool and Birkenhead Docks to a new body to be known as the Mersey Docks & Harbour Board and this came into effect on January 1st 1858. New engineers were engaged and Birkenhead Docks were extensively rebuilt and improved but not fully operational until the 1870s. For the remainder of the nineteenth century trade expanded rapidly and this continued into the twentieth century with new docks opened in 1909 (Vittoria) and 1933 (Bidston). All these docks were rail connected with peak tonnage reached during the Second World War.

A slow decline started in the 1960s due to changing patterns of trade and this continued during the 1970s and 80s with many quays becoming unused and derelict. The Mersey Docks &

BIRKENHEAD FLYOVERS

A Class '47' heads south out of Haymarket Tunnel leaving the centre of Birkenhead behind with a loaded coal train, during an eight month period of importation from Bidston Dock to Fiddler's Ferry Power Station in 1986. The tracks here at Blackpool Street had been reduced to only two from the former numerous lines. In the foreground is the connection leading to Mollington Street shed. *Richard Hambly*

Harbour Board continued until 1972 when it was reconstituted as the Mersey Docks & Harbour Company to raise funds for new works including the Seaforth Container Terminal in Liverpool; the company was bought by Peel Ports Ltd in 2005. While rail traffic from Birkenhead Docks ceased in 1993 the docks are still currently in operation and on a particular day in August 2020 three vessels were discharging cargo, with several service vessels also present and nearby, the Stena ferry terminal to Belfast.

Shortly after leaving Haymarket Tunnel a view looking south, from a DMU special 'The Mersey Mariner' on 26th November 1983, of the flyovers outside the toll plaza of the Queensway road tunnel. The curved flyover in the foreground is unfinished and remains so to this day but the track bed and general area are now completely covered by vegetation.
David Southern

By August 1985 the Docks Extension line looks rather neglected as shunter No. 03162 passes the photographer at Marion Street with a single tank wagon, south towards Rock Ferry. The last movement between Birkenhead North and Rock Ferry occurred in May 1993.
Richard Hambly

THE SOUGH

In May 1985, a pair of Class '25's at the same location, with a train of empty Grainflow wagons returning to Whitemoor Yard in March, Cambridgeshire. This section of track has a steep gradient of 1 in 100 rising towards Green Lane. *Richard Hambly*

Class '47' No. 47364 is seen on the Docks Extension line on 12th April 1986 with a train of imported coal from Bidston Dock to Fiddler's Ferry Power Station heading south. The train which ran for only an eight month period, has just gone under the bridge at the junction of Market Street and Adelphi Street. The cars piled up in the scrap yard above the train are dangerously close to the parapet and hopefully were well secured. *David Southern Collection*

BROOK STREET

Looking towards Grange Lane and Rock Ferry, Brook Street signal box on the dock extension railway was an L&NWR special narrow design, being just 8ft wide to fit in the 10ft between the pairs of lines. It housed a 30 lever tumbler frame and closed on 17th October 1973. The slate roof of the signal box had been replaced with roofing felt, possibly as a result of vandalism in this vulnerable location. The line to the docks is in a cutting supported by substantial brickwork retaining walls to reduce the area of land required as it passed through the town close to both residential and commercial properties.

Steve Weatherley

A GWR 'Grange' thought to be No. 6854 *Roundhill Grange*, reverses over the crossover between the two goods lines in front of Brook Street signal box in the 1950s. It is likely that the locomotive would be returning to Mollington Street shed after depositing a train in the docks. The fireman is leaning on the cab side looking out. During World War 2 congestion of the docks led to a build-up of wagons in this area but by the time of this photograph the quadruple track had been reduced to double, south of Brook Street.

Brian Elliot Collection

Viewed from Brook Street on 10th June 1967, a pair of Class '9F' 2-10-0s, No. 92011 leading No. 92159, have passed beneath Cleveland Street and about to pass the signal box on their way to Mollington Street depot. Due to the depot turntable being unavailable, the locomotives had visited Bidston triangle to the west to turn before taking up their next duties; almost all locomotives leaving Birkenhead depot faced south. The photographer had a patient two hours awaiting their return having seen them go north earlier. At an earlier time incoming freight trains reversed into the holding sidings (former through lines) on the left for onward distribution. The tracks diverging to the left led to Canning Street North with those on the right leading to Morpeth Dock and the CLC goods yard in Shore Road.

Barry Shore

The concrete hut next to the steps of Brook Street signal box housed the 'Elsan' toilet; note the horseshoe attached to the door with the coal bunker in the foreground. Brook Street ceased to function as a junction in September 1972, with closure the following year. *David Hill*

A PORTION OF THE MERSEY DOCK ESTATE AT BIRKENHEAD.

An aerial view of Birkenhead Docks circa 1930. The goods coming through it passed mainly onto the GW, LM&S and L&NER (previously GW, L&NW, and GCR) with some traffic filtering also down to the Wirral Railway. Birkenhead North Goods and the locomotive depot can be seen in the right foreground, partially obscured by the word 'Birkenhead'. The line performs a shallow 'S' as it runs on past and along Beaufort Road, a short way down which was the boundary with the Mersey Docks & Harbour Board. At the other end of Beaufort Road can just be made out the great fan of sorting sidings. In the left foreground is Wallasey Pool or Poulton Bridge and in the middle distance beyond that can be seen Wallasey Gas Works, with the electricity works just visible in front. The Great Float West runs through the centre of the view, with Duke Street swing bridge (in the open position) visible centre left, whilst Vittoria Dock can be seen in the centre background.
Neil Parkhouse Collection

Chapter Three
BIRKENHEAD DOCKS

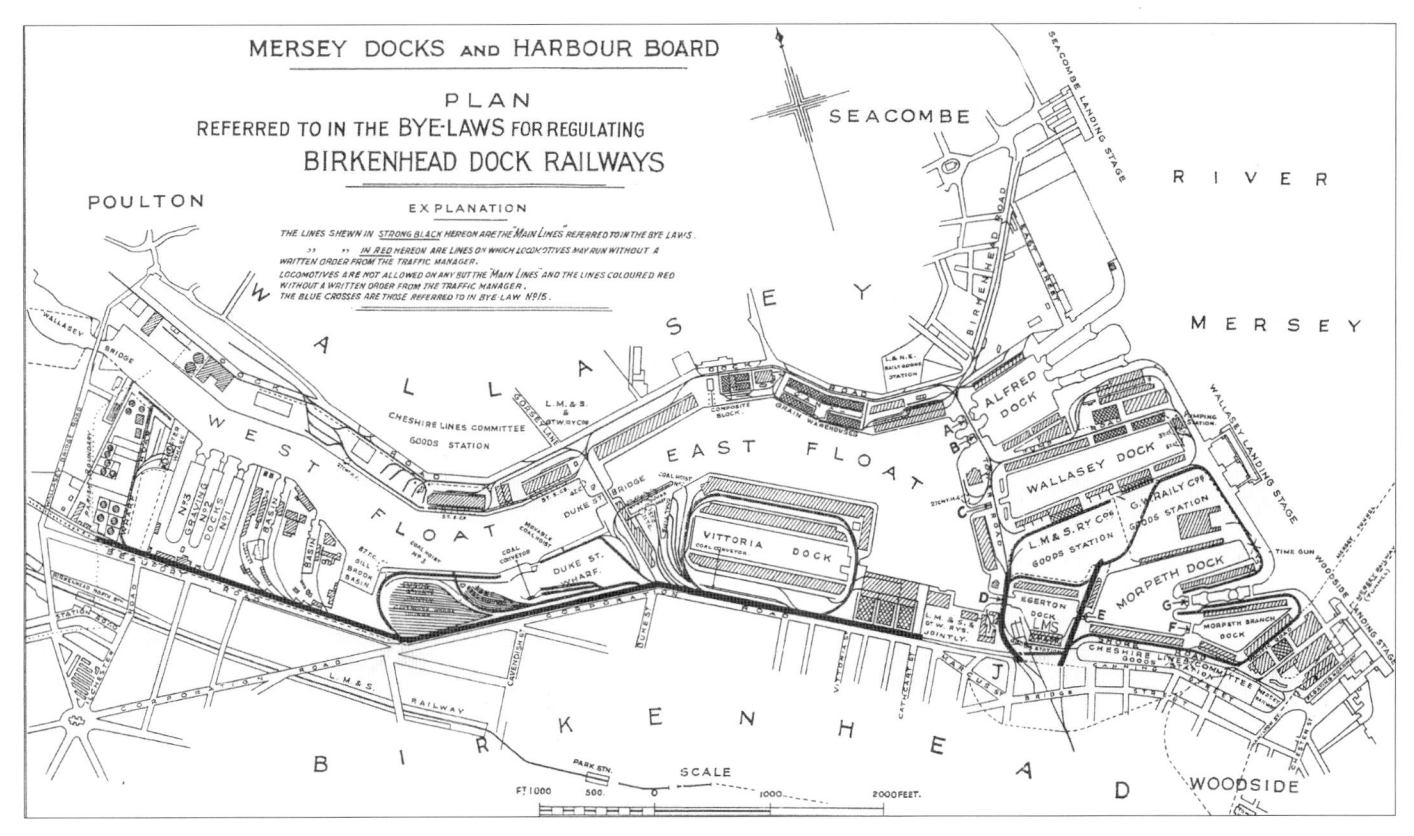

The Birkenhead Docks Extension Railway is on the bottom right of this plan and was the primary route for accessing the docks. The docks and the railways shown on this plan belonged to the Mersey Docks & Harbour Board and the next two chapters are concerned with these lines. The docks themselves in this chapter, with Chapter 4 covering the line running on the southern periphery of the docks known as the 'Cross-Dock' route.

INDUSTRIAL LOCOMOTIVES IN BIRKENHEAD DOCKS
There were three companies operating in Birkenhead Docks: -

WILLIAM J. LEE, Haulage Contractors
The Lee family appears to have been involved in the use of horses for haulage in the docks from as early as 1854. Their railway operations started around 1885, initially shunting in many of the smaller companies' premises and then expanding to serve larger operations like the grain and cattle wharves. They had their own fleet of locomotives until 1940, after which date they started using hired enignes. Their shed was in Seacombe just north of Alfred Dock. They continued operations until 1971.

JOSEPH PERRIN AND SON LTD Haulage Contractors
Perrins started haulage on the docks in 1891 and were similar to Lees but mainly serving the smaller companies in the dock estate. They always owned their own locomotives and their engine shed was in a corner of the CLC yard. They remained in business until 1969.

REA BULK HANDLING LTD
Rea's railway business started around 1900 with the operation of the Monks Ferry coaling wharf providing bunker coal for steam tugs until 1961. However their main business was at the Great Float where they were Master Porters and stevedores in bulk trades, particularly coal which was handled at the Duke Street Wharf, also known as Cavendish Wharf. In the late 1880s they were using their own fleet of coastal vessels to bring coal from South Wales to Birkenhead, to be used for bunkering cargo ships.

Rea's jetty started handling iron ore in the 1950s following the establishment of an open-hearth steel plant at the John Summers' works in Shotton, Flintshire. This traffic transferred to Bidston Dock in the mid-1950s after special cranes had been built for ore handling but this trade finished in 1980 after the end of steelmaking at Summers' plant. This was virtually the end for Rea's operations, although there was a brief revival in the mid-1980s due to coal for Fiddlers Ferry Power Station, being imported though Bidston Dock. Rea ceased operation around the mid-1980s when BR took over the remaining work.

SHORE STREET

Ex-North London 0-6-0T, now in LMS livery and renumbered No. 27528 (later 58861 under British Railways), is seen at the entrance to the CLC Yard in Shore Street in the 1930s. Note the Maudsley lorry on the left having just crossed over the bascule bridge at the east end of Egerton Dock. It is assumed that the locomotive is propelling its wagons into the yard, rather than hauling! *Glyn Parry Collection*

Pre-grouping variety at Birkenhead Docks in the 1930s sees L&NWR 0-4-2T No. 6402 attached to North Staffordshire Brake van No. 93508 at an unknown location in the docks. This locomotive was one of 20 in the L&NWR '317' Class built between 1896 and 1901 at Crewe. This engine was one of the few renumbered into the passenger sequence before being renumbered again into the goods series in 1927, so the picture must date between 1923 and 1927. *Glyn Parry Collection*

Birkenhead, a 0-4-0ST built by Manning Wardle, was supplied new to Joseph Perrin & Son in 1906 and is seen in the CLC Shore Road Yard in the late 1940s, before being scrapped in 1950. *Glyn Parry Collection*

Dock Shunter No. 47006 is shunting wagons in Shore Road in the 1950s. This class of enignes was known as 'Kitson tanks' as the first five were built by private locomotive builders, Kitson in Leeds, for the LMS in 1932. However No. 47006 was initially allocated to Birkenhead and was part of a second batch built by BR at Horwich in 1953 with shorter and deeper saddle tanks, small side tanks and increased coal capacity. *J.A.Peden/IRS*

The elderly 0-4-0ST seen shunting in the CLC yard in the early 1950s was *Cyclops*, a Hudswell Clarke locomotive built in 1895 for the Royal Arsenal at Woolwich. It was sold in 1920 to Currie Rowlands & Co. fertiliser manufacturers of Seacombe. By 1926 it was on hire to the MDHB for construction work at Bidston Dock. After further use by the MDHB in Liverpool it was sold to Cudworth & Johnson in 1947, was on hire to Lees by 1949 who used it in Birkenhead until 1961, it was scrapped in 1964. Note the spark arrester assembly over the chimney. *Glyn Parry Collection*

An Andrew Barclay 0-4-0ST 'Perrin 820' of 1898 belonging to Joseph Perrrin stands outside Shore Road Loco shed in the 1950s.
Harry Leadbetter Collection

SHORE ROAD ENGINE SHED

Shore Road, the smallest of Birkenhead's three locomotive depots, was opened by the Cheshire Lines Committee in 1888 and was located to the west of Shore Road Goods Depot. It was a single road timber built shed, 90 feet long with a pitched roof. The coal ramp and water crane were mainly used by dock shunting locomotives as well as visiting engines which had worked from the Wrexham – Bidston line. These visiting locomotives were serviced at the depot rather than returning to Bidston shed to avoid the cost of the MDHB tolls for passing over the Cross-Dock line.

The first locomotives to be allocated to Shore Road was a Manchester Sheffield & Lincolnshire Railway 0-4-0ST. When the L&NER took over Shore Road it became a sub-shed of Wrexham Rhosddu and J62 tanks were allocated there. On nationalisation Shore Road became a sub-shed of Bidston and continued to be used by ex-L&NER and GCR locomotives. Shunting engines belonging to Joseph Perrin & Son Ltd also used the shed under a sharing arrangement. The use of the shed gradually declined and the last locomotive allocated there was withdrawn in October 1960. The CLC goods shed closed in June 1961 which ended the need for the locomotive shed which was also closed, but Perrin's locomotives continued using the shed until the end of their tenancy

A view of Shore Road shed on 22nd October 1961 with one of Perrin's locomotives outside. *Roger Carpenter*

A Cheshire Lines Committee label used for wagon sheets, in this case from Shore Road to Stockport CLC, otherwise known as Tiviot Dale. The label seems to date from 1940; the Cheshire Lines Committee was not subject to the 1923 grouping, continuing in joint LMS/L&NER ownership until nationalisation in 1948.

A close up view of Shore Road shed in 1967 showing the dilapidated state of its later days.
John Cashen

MORPETH DOCK

GWR 4-6-0 4921 *Eaton Hall* departs from Morpeth Dock with a Class '4' fitted freight in the 1950s having crossed Egerton Bridge. The GWR style ATC equipment is prominent below the buffers in this view, such apparatus was vulnerable to damage from the cobbled surface in the docks area. *A. Williams*

A Class '25' No. D5202 negotiates the bridge between Egerton and Morpeth Docks with a van train around 1970. In the background an Austin A35 in front of the warehouse between Shore Road and Morpeth Dock. The 5H at the start of the headcode would indicate a partly-fitted train towards Manchester. The working time table of 1968 shows a 17.44 light engine from Chester depot to Morpeth Dock (arrive 18.44) to work this train.
Pacer Archives

A GWR Class '47XX' 2-8-0 weaves its way out of the docks across the bridge passing the entrance to Shore Road CLC Goods Yard (the tracks to the right passing under the footbridge) in the 1950s. The lines to the left went to Canning Street Junction and the lines to the right to Brook Street. The footbridge span is now a plate girder rather than the latticework seen earlier.
A. Williams

Late on a summer evening GWR 'Heavy Freight' 2-8-0 No. 4704 leaves Morpeth Yard and crosses the bridge at the western end of Morpeth Dock (known as Bridge E) with mixed freight of vans and open wagons. The shed plate, 81A, indicates that the locomotive is allocated to Old Oak Common in London which places the photograph between 1951 and 1962, the locomotive having previously been allocated to Birkenhead. It was last noted in Birkenhead in 1963 working the 8.20 pm Birkenhead to Paddington goods known as 'The General'.
A. Williams

Leaving the same bascule bridge is GWR No. 4079 *Pendennis Castle* on the dock railway system with a van freight in this 1950s view. 'Castle' Class locomotives were not common in Birkenhead Docks but were seen after withdrawal of the 47xx locomotives in early 1960s. Shore Street is to the right of the picture with the skewed dock side steps leading to the footbridge.
A. Williams

Late on a summer evening GWR 4-6-0 No. 6963 *Throwley Hall* is seen with the bascule bridge between Egerton and Morpeth Docks before working a freight for Chester in the late 1950s. *Throwley Hall* was allocated to Chester (West) shed between 1952 and 1958.
A. Williams

Another one of the BR built Kitson Tanks, No. 47009, is seen at Morpeth Dock on 25th March 1957. This was initially allocated to Birkenhead where it remained until its only move to Agecroft in 1963, from where it was withdrawn the following year. *Jon Penn Collection*

In the early 1970s No. D5034 arrives at Morpeth Dock to pick up its next working. The tracks in this area are now surrounded by concrete, replacing the cobbles seen in earlier views. The line to the left led to the north side of Egerton Dock and the 'Four Bridges' route back to Canning Street. Morpeth Dock Goods Station closed in 1972 after handling little during the previous months. *Pacer Archives*

The same Class '24' is seen in Morpeth Yard waiting for instructions from the shunters whilst a Class '03' shunts the yard in the 1970s. The former stables are seen in the centre of the photograph with the Liver Building across the river in the background.
Pacer Archives

Class '03' shunter No. D2374 propels loaded cattle wagons into Morpeth Dock Yard, having brought the train from Morpeth Lairage and reversed at Shore Road. The photograph was most probably taken during its two years allocated to Birkenhead from September 1961. The locomotive has yellow/black ('wasp') warning stripes on the rear. Cattle was a substantial part of the docks' traffic for many decades, principally from Ireland, until the decline started in 1967 with the removal of the cattle landing stage. In the 1970s the traffic was only a trickle and by 1980 it had ceased. Around this date all goods traffic was concentrated on Morpeth Yard with trains assembled in Morpeth West Sidings. *Pacer Archives*

Hudswell-Clarke 0-6-0 diesel shunter No. 11144 is seen working at the throat of Morpeth Dock Yard. Their design still resembled a steam locomotives with a chimney and rear bunker. This type of locomotive was the first diesel type in the docks being successfully tested in April 1956. The locomotive was new to Birkenhead the following month and was renumbered as D2505 in 1960. The vessel at the wharf is one of the Isle of Man Steam Packet Company's ships laid up for the winter. *Jon Penn Collection*

A GWR Armstrong '1901' Class pannier tank No. 1949 is seen at rest in Morpeth Dock in the 1940s. On the siding behind the locomotive, porters are busy loading vans from road vehicles in the days before fork lift trucks and other mechanical handling equipment. During World War 2 the docks were very busy, with the African campaigns largely supplied from Birkenhead.
E.C.Lloyd Collection

GWR 4-6-0 No. 4943 *Marrington Hall* waits to leave Morpeth Dock Yard with a mixed freight in this early 1950s scene. Worthy of note are the tall funnelled ships in the adjacent dock and also in the corner of the dock is a laid up Wallasey ferry.
Jon Penn Collection

In Morpeth Dock Yard in the late 1950s, is a Stanier 2-6-4T with a fitted van train. The loading berth is in the foreground with the Goods Station to the rear. The dock was reconstructed in 1930 to eliminate barge loading berths within the warehouse so increasing the number of sidings, both inside and out. This was part of the major effort by the GWR to gain a share of the Liverpool goods traffic. The GWR concentrated its freight service in one location, unlike the LMS which had three separate sites.
Pacer Archives

The tug *Anita Lamey* is seen in the locks between the River Mersey and the Alfred Dock Basin which opened in 1866; in the background are the 'Three Graces'. The firm of J.H. Lamey was founded in 1916 and operated on the Mersey until 1968 when it was taken over by Alexandra Towing. The company were well known for operating second hand tugs. *Anita Lamey* was built in 1920 and originally named *Thunderer*. Bought by Lameys in 1952 it was renamed and served until 1967, with the picture taken near the end of its life.

Alan Southern

Against the backdrop of the Liverpool Waterfront's iconic 'Three Graces', two Mersey tugs await entrance into Birkenhead docks in the 1960s. The more modern tug on the right, Maple Garth, bears a white letter R in a black diamond on its funnel, indicating that it is part of the fleet operated by Rea Bulk Handling. The left hand tug, Trafalgar, belonged to Alexendra Towing Company. Above the left hand tug is the roof of Liverpool Riverside station.
Alan Southern

Blue Funnel Line cargo liner, *MS Melanpus*, is manoeuvring to enter Birkenhead Docks from the Mersey in this mid-1960s view. It is just possible to make out a tow line attached to the bow of the ship, while the tug in the foreground, William Lamey, is preparing to attach to the stern. The Melampus was part of the 'Yellow Fleet' which was trapped in the Suez Canal when it closed between 1967 and 1975 due to the Israel-Egypt conflicts.

Alan Southern

A classic view of '8F' No. 48351 with a Class '5' van train in Morpeth Dock Yard in the 1960s and the Liver Building on the Liverpool shore framed by the loading gauge. The buildings to the left were the warehouses on the south quay of Wallasey Dock. This area is now in use as roll-on/roll-off port facility for services to Belfast.

Richard Thomson/ Online Photo Archive

Churchward GWR heavy freight locomotive No.4704 swings round the curve from Morpeth Dock with an express freight, probably the 7.45 pm to Royal Oak (Paddington) and joins the cobbled streets of the dock estate in the 1950s. Under the 1861 lease to operate the docks, the MDHB were obliged to provide convenient rail lines in the docks so Birkenhead was unusual in permitting the usage of main line locomotives on the quayside. The Great Western Railway was able to attract traffic from Liverpool by using carts on the goods ferry across the Mersey before putting them on to fast trains to the likes of Bristol and London. The goods ferry closed in 1947 diverting traffic to the road tunnel under the Mersey. This illogical method lasted until 1951 when Birkenhead came under the sole control of the London Midland Region who correctly dispatched goods directly from Liverpool.
A.Williams

The Egerton bascule bridge (marked E on the plan) was built for the MDHB in 1932 by Sir William Arrol and Co. of Glasgow, builders of the Forth Bridge. In this 1980s view the rail tracks have been lifted and many of the warehouses demolished, however the bridge has been preserved as part of the areas heritage and the road network. The scene is almost unrecognisable due to much redevelopment.
David Hill

FOUR BRIDGES

L&NWR Ramsbottom Special saddle tank No. 7291 takes water near a City Line warehouse on Tower Road in the 1930s with a runner's wagon behind. In 1892 City Line Ltd ran a fortnightly cargo and passenger service to Calcutta from Liverpool and a monthly cargo and passenger service to Bombay and Karachi. In 1901 it was acquired by London, Liverpool & Ocean Shipping Co. Ltd and its name changed to Ellerman City Line Ltd. *Glyn Parry Collection*

At the same location, a former Midland Railway Johnson Class '1F' half-cab 0-6-0T receives attention from its crew; while an industrial 0-4-0 saddle tank is shunting wagons in the 1930s at the throat of the former L&NWR yard at South Reserve. *Glyn Parry Collection*

A member of the '2021' Class of GWR open cab pannier tank locomotives shunts in Tower Road with its warning bell in full swing. A member of this class, No. 2069, was the last GWR locomotive to be allocated at Birkenhead in 1959. The track to the right leads to Canning Street signal box.

Note the Austin car parked by the distinctively angular shaped warehouse on the left. In the 1930s Birkenhead had become a generally export location, with the exception of meat traffic. Ships used to offload in Liverpool then crossed the river to be loaded with goods from Birkenhead. *E.C.Lloyd Collection*

A common sight in Birkenhead but very strange elsewhere, was a train running up the middle of the main road. *Hudswell Clarke* 0-6-0 No. 11119 is seen approaching Bridge 'D' on the 'Four Bridges' route on Tower Road in the late 1950s with a cattle wagon heading over the docks to Wallasey. The locomotive was new to Birkenhead in 1956 and withdrawn in 1967. The car in front of the locomotive was a Standard Vanguard or Ensign with the view taken in the same location as the previous photograph.
Edgar Richards/Jon Penn Collection

Typical of Birkenhead Docks in the 1960s; a coaster under tow from the tug *Collingwood* has passed through Tower Road swing bridge and is in Alfred Dock heading for the Mersey, with a second ship following. On the extreme right is a laid-up Mersey ferry in Mortar Mill Quay in the East Float, while on the left is the large tower which gave its name to Tower Road. The tower was actually an accumulator for the hydraulic system installed in 1863 to operate lock gates and bridges in the dock complex. The 110 foot high tower was designed by renowned dock engineer Jesse Hartley and was supposedly based on the Palazzo Vecchio in Florence. To the left of the tower is the jib of the heavy lift crane '*Mammoth*'.
Alan Southern

EGERTON DOCK

A variety of wagons in Egerton Dock are seen, as a GWR 'Mogul' passes light engine probably bound for Mollington Street shed around 1957. The photograph was taken from Bridge Street with Canning Street to the left. Note the van with the tarpaulin covering in the background, no doubt because of a leaking roof.
Glyn Parry Collection

Another open cab pannier tank, this time No. 1968 of the '1901' Class, built in Wolverhampton in 1890 originally as a saddle tank, is seen in the beginning of the 1950s with painted British Railways markings on the tank before. It was withdrawn in 1951 with the last two examples of this class withdrawn from Birkenhead seven years later. On this locomotives the warning bell is mounted between the dome and the chimney. Note also the horse dray on the left with its shafts in a vertical position. The picture is taken to the south of the warehouse on the south side of Egerton Dock; Canning Street signal box is in the background with the lattice girder footbridge over the level crossing just visible. *Glyn Parry Collection*

CANNING STREET NORTH

Class '47' No. 47356 approaches Canning Street North signal box with a Whitemoor Yard to Cavendish Sidings Grainflow working in the 1980s. The line to the left of the box was the start of the through Cross-Dock route which went round the periphery of the docks, rejoining BR metals at Wallasey Bridge Road. The lines to the right gave access to the 'Four Bridges' route and the former South Reserve. This area was initially known as 'Bridge End' and was the first terminus of the 1.25 mile Birkenhead Docks Extension Railway from Grange Lane. This section of the line was opened 5th April 1847, a date which coincided with the opening of Birkenhead Docks, and Birkenhead Park laid out by Paxton. *David Southern Collection*

A Class '47' passes over Canning Street North Crossing in the 1980s. Note the red and amber warning lights for road traffic, installed to supplement the crossing gates at this busy road junction. On the right is the land formerly used for the connection to Egerton Dock Goods Depot, seen previously in the 1924 photograph. This area was a source of much dispute in the 1860s as it was on the boundary between the railway and the MDHB lines with the footbridge and crossing opening in 1872. *David Hill*

A 1924 official photograph showing the busy scene at the former L&NWR Egerton Dock Goods Warehouse with Canning Street signal box on the right. The lines to the left went to the 'Four Bridges' route. The numerous horse drays surrounding the railway wagons are in various stages of loading, while most of the porters have posed for the photographer. Maps from that period show no less than 24 wagon turntables to the side and front of this warehouse. The masts of several ships are visible in Egerton Dock. Egerton Dock warehouse was damaged during World War 2 with this end of the building being demolished. For many years a grounded coach body served as the foreman's office. The warehouse officially closed in June 1961 but is still standing after refurbishment into office accommodation.

National Railway Museum

The same view of Canning Street North signal box but 60 years later in the 1980s shows the dramatic decline of the dock estate, with land near the box becoming derelict. The signal box was built in 1900. The drastic reduction in rail traffic meant that the signalman had a lot of spare time on his hands which he used to create an 'urban garden' next to the box. He must have been fond of streamlined 'Pacifics' as the numbers painted in the background are of L&NER *Silver Link* and LMS *Coronation* locomotives. The line curving away to the right is the BR line to Rock Ferry while the other two routes are MDHB lines into the dock estate, both out of use by this time. This scene is almost unrecognisable with only the battered remains of the road traffic signals and a gate remaining to indicate the location.   *David Hill*

An enthusiasts' railtour, 'The Wirral & Mersey Special' from Liverpool to Manchester, organised by the Liverpool University Public Transport Society, headed by LMS 2-6-0 No. 42942 approaches Canning Street signal box from the Rock Ferry direction on 22nd October 1966. The locomotive was about to enter on to Mersey Docks and Harbour Board metals and was the last 'Crab' on the Wirral leaving in January 1967. In the background is the ventilation station for the former Rendel Street branch of the Mersey Tunnel.   *Edgar Richards/Jon Penn Collection*

With an excess of steam Class '9F' 2-10-0 No. 92224 has just joined BR metals at Canning Street North with a Class '8' train of mineral wagons in the mid-1960s, watched by the stationmaster from Birkenhead North who was paying the box a visit at the time. The locomotive lamp irons had moved to suit electrification with the upper bracket lowered and the middle buffer beam bracket sited directly underneath. The cleared lower signal indicates the route going round to the right i.e. towards Brook Street.
Glyn Parry Collection

The interior of Canning Street North signal box is seen on 18th August 1981. In the foreground is the 18 lever L&NWR tumbler frame with a block instrument and signal repeater on the shelf above. In the background can be seen the gas fired water heater, and the large enamel sink. This type of sink was known as a 'Belfast' sink and was based on design dating from the 1700s. Originally installed in large country houses, they became widely used in commercial premises in the twentieth century, with BR fitting them in signal boxes from the 1950s. *Trefor Thompson*

Chapter Four
MERSEY DOCKS AND HARBOUR BOARD - THE 'CROSS-DOCK' ROUTE.

The diagram shows the extensive railway connections to the many docks and wharves, as well as the Cross-Dock route round the periphery of Birkenhead Docks to the north of Corporation Road. The through route started at Canning Street North and ran parallel to Corporation and Beaufort Roads before crossing Wallasey Bridge Road on the level and forming a junction with the Wirral Railway just west of its docks locomotive depot.

The MDHB charged a toll for wagons passing over its line to reach factories, while those discharging at wharves were exempt and this caused many disputes over the years. However the construction materials brought in over this route for the many new factories were exempt from paying the toll to encourage future income. From the 1950s the line provided a convenient route for locomotives going from Mollington Street shed to Bidston Dock to work iron ore trains to Shotton Steelworks. Whilst the first section of the route, adjacent to Corporation Road was hidden behind a brick wall, the section alongside Beaufort Road was open which made it a good location for photography.

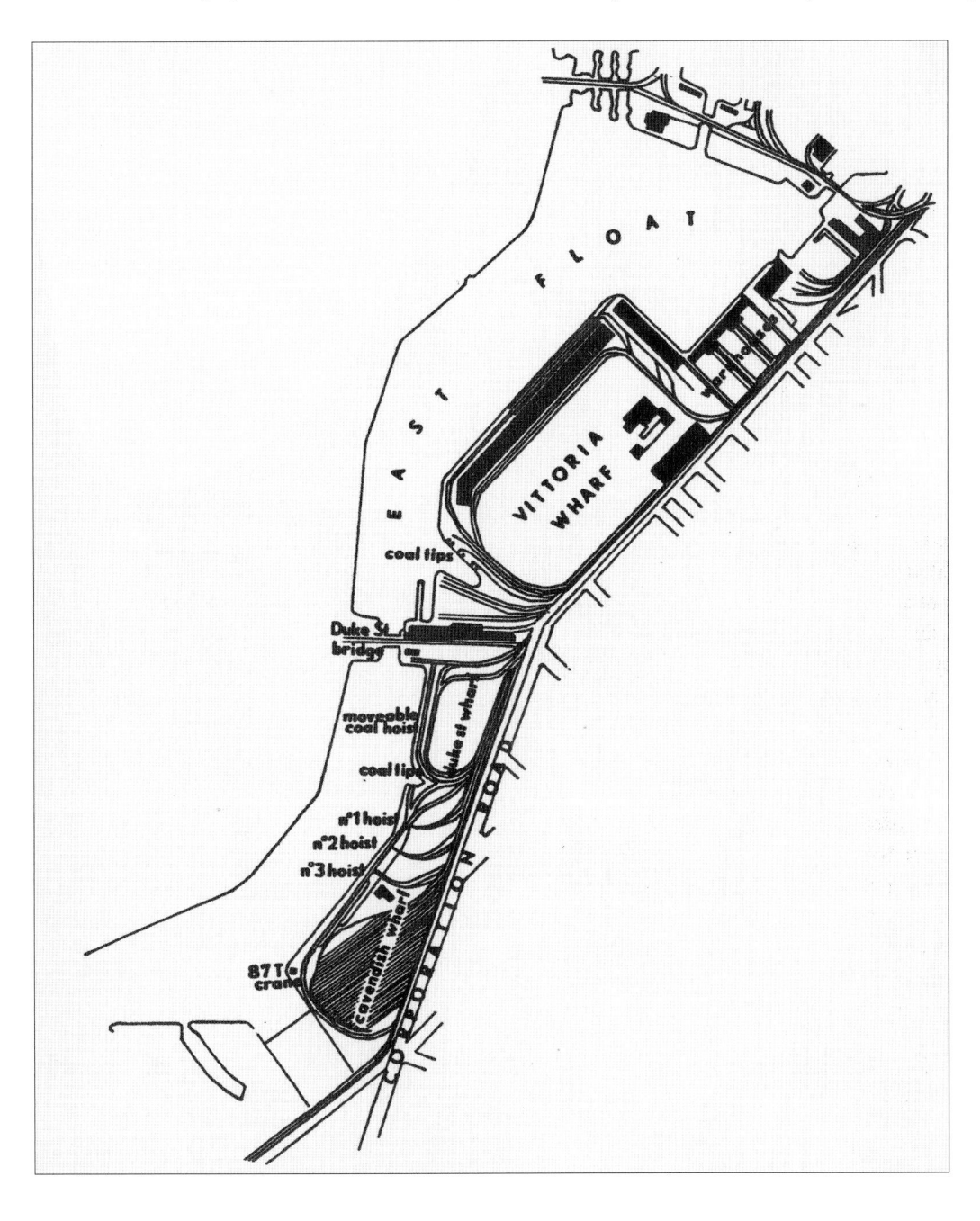

CATHCART STREET GOODS DEPOT

Midland 1F 0-6-0T No. 41734, hauling a short rake of wagons, joins the Cross-Dock Railway from Cathcart Street Goods Depot near Canning Street North on 25th March 1957. The locomotive was allocated to Birkenhead at nationalisation and left in 1958. Cathcart Street depot was devoid of development in the first half of the twentieth century with numerous Dickensian offices still lit by gas. The depot officially closed in June 1961, along with Egerton Dock and Shore Street depots, leaving all traffic handled at Morpeth Dock. *Authors' Collection*

The joint ownership of Cathcart Street Goods Depot is proudly proclaimed though it was by then a purely LMS facility. This view taken around 1924 shows the great variety and volume of goods handled then. The porters on the left standing on the horse dray have paused in their labours for the photographer. Worthy of note is the six wheel brake van in the centre foreground which is of L&NWR origin. *National Railway Museum*

In the 1980s a Class '47' hauls empty grain wagons past the new road access to Cathcart Street Wharf which opened in the early 1970s. The open area behind the locomotive was the site of the former Cathcart Street Goods Depot. *David Southern*

A locomotive hauled railtour, 'The Birkenhead Bandit', organised by Lea Valley Railway Club headed by a Class '40' D200 No. 40106 is seen approaching Canning Street North on 16th February 1985. The train is crossing the road that accessed Cathcart Street lorry park and is passing from the MDHB lines onto BR metals. Strangely, the barrier protecting Cathcart Street crossing is in the raised position despite the signal having been cleared for the train which should not have been possible. In the background are two laid-up Isle of Man ferries showing the severe decline in shipping traffic from Birkenhead. *David Southern*

There was a continuous need for dredging in the docks to remove the mud and silt which accumulated by the wharves. In August 1985 we see a large dredger operating in the exit of Vittoria Dock leading into the East Float. Framed on either side of the dredger are two landmarks on the Liverpool side of the Mersey, These being the Roman Catholic Cathedral on the left and the Anglican Cathedral on the right.
Richard Hambly

VITTORIA DOCK

DUKE STREET

In 1931 a new bascule bridge was installed at Duke Street to replace an earlier swing bridge; this bridge separating the East and West Floats. In this view the bridge is being tested by standing a number of steam locomotives on it. Visible are a GWR '66XX' tank on the left and an L&NWR Class 'G1' 0-8-0 on the right. To the left of the bridge is a Rea operated tug and one of their cranes for unloading iron ore. The bridge demonstration is being watched by a large crowd of dignitaries in their finest dress.
Glyn Parry Collection

Looking east from Duke Street on 18th January 1986 as two Class '33's, No. 33051 and No. 33062 haul the 'Wirral Widdershins' railtour from London Victoria which traversed the MDHB lines returning via Wrexham. The lines going left on the picture ran over Duke Street bridge and the lines under the photographers feet led to Cavendish Sidings. *David Southern*

The high dock wall to the west of Cathcart Street precluded photography and this view is taken at Duke Street crossing. A two-car 'Pacer' unit is seen approaching from the Canning Street direction with a Chester Depot to Bidston ECS working in the late 1980s, a method which lasted only for around six months. On arrival at Bidston the unit would take up service on the line to Wrexham Central. *David Hill*

In July 1985 one of Rea's 0-4-0 diesel locomotives leaves Duke Street Bridge heading for the Wallasey side of the docks to fulfil shunting contracts at the grain storage facilities on that side of the East Float. Note the two shunters riding on the footsteps and running board of the locomotive. The three cars visible were all British made with a Morris Ital, Vauxhall Chevette and Triumph Dolomite. *Richard Hambly*

A year later in 1986 and BR had taken over the remaining shunting duties on the docks, a Class '08' shunter is seen in the same location as the previous photo going to pick up empty grain wagons. Note the Foden lorry following the '08' off Duke Street bridge. Also the laid-up ships, seen earlier, are no longer in Vittoria Dock having been sold to new Greek owners. *Richard Hambly*

Birkenhead Docks had considerable goods traffic in the 19th & 20th centuries before it withered away in the 1980s. On 9th October 1987, No. 03170 has just crossed into Birkenhead over Duke Street bridge with a single empty grain wagon from the flour mills on the East Float in Wallasey.
David Pool

Four Cunard ships are laid up in Vittoria Dock in 1985 due to lack of work. The vessels were *Saxonia, Samaria, Carmania* and *Carinthia*. The row of neatly lined up cranes show that Vittoria Dock no longer had any commercial traffic by the 1980s.
David Hill

In the 1970s this wagon turntable was located near Duke Street Bridge. These turntables were commonly used all over the docks network to avoid points in cramped locations.
David Southern

Industrial locomotives *Efficient* (an 0-4-0ST built by Andrew Barclay in 1918, Works No. 1598 and *Lucy* (an 0-6-0ST built by Avonside in 1909, Works No. 1569) double head the Birkenhead Docker No. 3 railtour over Duke Street crossing on 1st July 1972. They are watched by the traffic policeman on his podium. This important person had control over both road and rail traffic and was a well known feature of the cross dock railway for many years. The two locomotives were owned by the Liverpool Locomotive Preservation group and are now located at the Ribble Steam Railway in Preston.
Adrian Bodlander

This 1980s view of Duke Street Crossing shows BR Tamping Machine No. DX 73274 passing over. The Royal Duke Hotel was still open although the local Birkenhead brewery has now been taken over by Whitbread, sadly the hotel has now been demolished.
David Hill

The Class '08's were soon found to be unsuitable for the sharp curves on the dock railway and their duties were taken over by Class '03's. Around 1987 No. 03162 is returning from the last remaining grain storage depot on the north side of the East Float over Duke Street bridge with three empty grain wagons and as the road sign helpfully points out, is heading for Cavendish Wharf. The locomotive is preserved under the ownership of Wirral Borough Council but is located at the Llangollen Railway. *Richard Hambly*

Ex-North London 0-6-0T No. 27513 (BR No. 58854) waits its turn to cross Duke Street in this 1930s view, whilst a Birkenhead Corporation bus operates a Wallasey to Birkenhead service; such conflicting movements were common at this location. Duke Street classified as the A5027 forms one of the main routes between Birkenhead and Wallasey.
Glyn Parry Collection

The use of elderly pre-grouping locomotives continued into the BR era, as shown in this early 1950s view of North London Bow Works built tank 58851 alongside an early Midland '1F' half-cab 0-6-0T. No. 58851 was withdrawn in November 1952 having returned to its home at Devons Road shed in London.
Glyn Parry Collection

In May 1948 Johnson '1F' 0-6-0 No.41853 newly painted in the first British Railways livery shunts near the road crossing on Duke Street. It was one of five such class members allocated to Birkenhead at nationalisation and withdrawn in October 1954. Note the traffic signal installed to assist the policeman at this location in controlling traffic.

N.N.Forbes/Glyn Parry Collection

'J94' Class 0-6-0ST No. 68065 crosses Duke Street on 5th April 1961 hauling a variety of wagons probably to Bidston Yard and passes the Royal Duke Hotel proudly advertising Birkenhead Ales.
Glyn Parry Collection

0-4-0ST *Homepride* was supplied new to Paul Brothers (a part of Spillers) in 1924, for use at their Seacombe Flour Mill; the owners taking pride in the good condition of the locomotive. It was owned by them until 1957 when it was sold to Cudworth & Johnson who hired it to Lees from 1958 to 1964. It is seen near Duke Street behind Corporation Road; Paul Brothers had another flour mill nearby on Beaufort Road for many decades. *Glyn Parry Collection*

'THE END OF THE LINE'. Five industrial locomotives from various manufacturers stand out of use at Duke Street in 1964, there being no further work for them.
Harry Leadbetter Collection

At the same location in June 1977, steam had been replaced by diesel. Three of Rea's shunters in their light blue livery are seen with the nearest locomotive being *Labrador*. This locomotive was a 0-4-0 built by Yorkshire Engine Co. as works number 2732 of 1959 to the same design as British Railways Class '02' but with electric rather than hydraulic traction, the only locomotive type built with a verandah.
David Southern

An LMS Fowler 0-6-0 dock tank is seen at West Float near Duke Street Wharf with a trip freight in the late 1940s, with the particular working shown by the number over the left hand buffer. Ten of this type were designed by Fowler and introduced 1928-1929. They were specifically designed for use in docks with driving wheels just less than 4 feet in diameter and capable of traversing a 100m radius curve because of fitting Cartazzi self-centring axleboxes to the rear axle.
Glyn Parry Collection

Melsonby No. 3 was a Manning Wardle 0-4-0ST dating from 1895. It was purchased by Cudworth & Johnson in 1946 and was hired by both Lees and Reas for several short periods between 1949 & 1954 and was scrapped in 1955.
Glyn Parry Collection

CAVENDISH SIDINGS

Class '24' No. 5063 passes Cavendish Sidings with a train of empty coal wagons from Birkenhead North Coal Depot on 28th February 1971. The conical tank in the background was used for the storage of dried goods.
David Southern

In April 1987 No. 03073 shunts vans in Cavendish Sidings with dockside cranes silhouetted against the skyline. The locomotive is preserved at the Crewe Heritage Centre, having been withdrawn in 1989 when the sidings closed. At this time Cavendish Sidings were the centre for the remaining traffic at the Docks. The flour mills on the south side of the West Float are visible in the background. *Richard Hambly*

Two Rea diesels are seen in Cavendish Wharf Sidings in the late 1960s. The right-hand one is *Theseus* built by Drewry/ Vulcan in 1951 and bought by Reas in 1959. The left hand locomotive is thought to be *W.H.Salthouse* built by Drewry/ Robert Stephenson & Hawthorn in 1959, and bought by Rea in 1960. It was loaned to Lees for a short period in 1966. In the background is again the conical store for dry powders. *David Southern*

Iron ore on the quayside at Cavendish Wharf waiting to be loaded into railway wagons in the 1970s. This wharf was the first to be used for iron ore however from 1955 specialised cranes were erected at Bidston Dock to handle the increasing tonnages going to the John Summers' works at Shotton. Cavendish Wharf continued to handle ore consigned to other plants such as Brymbo (Wrexham), Shelton (Staffs) and even Rotherham. *Alan Southern*

Amongst other materials handled by Cavendish Wharf was scrap iron and here a Rea's shunter in its light blue livery is almost obscured by a huge pile of crushed steel, cars perhaps, in the mid-1970s. *Alan Southern*

This late 1930s view of the Electric Coal Conveyor at Cavendish Wharf is a promotional post card issued by the Mersey Docks & Harbour Board and shows the extent of coal handling equipment at this time. The central tower ran on rails allowing for a variety of off-loading positions. 'Bunker' coal is being loaded onto the ship for its own boilers, while the private owner wagons in the foreground bear the names of eight different collieries or coal factors from England and Wales. These extensive sidings were provided by the MHDB in 1878 and closed in 1961. The locomotive, LMS 1893, was built in 1899 and withdrawn shortly after nationalisation without having gained a British Railways number. Although it was a LMS locomotive, it is accompanied by a GWR shunter's truck demonstrating the joint operation of these sidings. In the distance were the L&NER sidings at Vittoria Wharf, served by the collieries on the Wrexham - Hawarden line.
J.A.Peden/John Ryan Collection

A dilapidated and stripped Stanier '8F' 2-8-0 stands on a temporary section of track at Cavendish Wharf on 25th April 1948. Built by Beyer-Peacock in Manchester as No. 70402, it was delivered to the War Department in July 1940 for service overseas during World War 2. After returning to the UK it acquired the BR number 48287 in 1949 and remained in service until July 1967.
B.Roberts/J.A. Peden Collection/IRS

BEAUFORT ROAD

A special working in December 1986 of a Railfreight Class '47' hauling a Class '507' EMU with attendant barrier wagons, alongside Beaufort Road. The EMU was heading from Birkenhead North Depot for a heavy overhaul at a BR works, probably Horwich. *Richard Hambly*

On 24th March 1982 No. 03189 is seen propelling Polybulk grain wagons into Rank's Ocean Flour Mills on Beaufort Road. In the 1930s Merseyside was the second largest flour milling centre in the world, with the bulk of the mills located around the Great Float in Birkenhead and Wallasey. Ocean Flour Mill was initially constructed in 1912 but was severely damaged by bombing in World War 2 and subsequently rebuilt with a more modern structure. *Roy Fell*

A more detailed view of the operation inside the gate of Ocean Flour Mill is seen in August 1987 with a Class '03' shunter and grain wagons inside the cobbled yard having just passed over the weighbridge. At this time the operating company was Rank Hovis McDougal. *Richard Hambly*

The bulk carrier *Penchateau* is seen at the grain wharf on the West Float having discharged cargo for the adjacent Spillers Flour Mill between Canada and Rank's Creeks. The ship was built in 1976 and was lost on 20th February 1991 as the *Gallant Dragon* having hit a submerged object off Brazil. In this late 1970s view two members of the Liverpool Victoria Rowing Club are lifting sculls from the water; the club despite its name has always been based on the Great Float in Birkenhead.

Alan Southern

Trainload Coal liveried No. 37235 is passing Rank's Ocean Flour Mills on Beaufort Road with empties from Birkenhead North Coal Concentration Depot in the late 1980s, when three trains a week were running to Washwood Heath in Birmingham. This working, later to South Wales, was the last surviving freight on Birkenhead Docks, lasting until February 1993. The last recorded working on the dock lines was of a Class '08' shunter on 10th May 1993.

David Hill

Two Class '33's, No.33051 and 3No.3062 haul the 'Wirral Widdershins' railtour on 18th January 1986 over the Cross-Dock route alongside Beaufort Road, with the rear of the train turning from Corporation Road. The traverse of the dock lines was achieved in 27 minutes, a third of the booked time and the train ran over an hour early to Wrexham.
David Southern

On the open section of the Cross-Dock route, alongside Beaufort Road, a Class '8F' 2-8-0 is seen with a van train in the 1960s, possibly from Cadburys at Moreton. In the foreground is a British Transport Advertising Vauxhall Viva van while the two large cranes serve Bidston Graving Docks. In the background the three iron ore cranes at Bidston Dock are visible.
David Southern Collection

In the 1960s just a little further west along Beaufort Road a van train is seen, hauled by a Class '3F' 0-6-0T, known as a *Jinty*. On Beaufort Road a Birkenhead bus is operating a service on route 90, from Wallasey to Woodside. At this time there was housing along the south side of the road, around Lincoln Street; it is now the 'Park and Ride' parking area for Birkenhead North station. *K.Longbottom/Harry Leadbetter Collection*

A special working seen on Beaufort Road in May 1985 was this inspection saloon hauled by a Class '47' heading for Birkenhead North and the Mersey electric lines. *Richard Hambly*

A little further west on Beaufort Road in December 1987 shunter No. 03170 is seen passing the graving docks with a trip working of coal wagons from Cavendish Sidings to Birkenhead North Coal Concentration Depot. The Spillers and Rank flour mills are in the distance. The small building behind the train is still present offering a landmark to guide a visitor to the area. *Richard Hambly*

Class '40' D200 No.40106 in BR green livery hauls 'The Birkenhead Bandit' railtour on a slightly snowy 16th February 1985 across Wallasey Bridge Road and onto MDHB metals at the start of the Cross-Dock route. The bunkers of the coal depot can be seen above the first three coaches, with Birkenhead North Electric Traction Depot out of shot to the left. The tracks swinging right gave access to the Mobil oil works and then crossed Wallasey Bridge Road by a second crossing at an angle before reaching Bidston Dock. The building in the background is the former refuse incinerator, the site now a recycling centre. *David Southern*

Chapter Five
MERSEY AND WIRRAL RAILWAYS
ROCK FERRY TO BIRKENHEAD NORTH

For centuries crossing the Mersey had been by ferry and the Grange Lane terminus was near to three equally distant ferry terminals. However there was a growing demand for a fixed crossing, either a rail tunnel or road bridge. In 1865 the first scheme for the construction of the Birkenhead & Liverpool Railway using pneumatic propulsion failed on technical grounds and to the L&NWR wishing to retain a monopoly on Liverpool traffic. In 1866 another scheme based on the earlier one suggested a road/rail bridge of 38 spans, equally failed.

Due to poor trading conditions it was not until 1868 when the promoters obtained an extension of time and with the name of the undertaking changing to the Mersey Railway, an Act of Parliament was obtained in 1871. This provided for a steam-worked double-track tunnel with the first sod being cut on the 29th December 1879; the delay being due to financial and engineering difficulties. The line between Liverpool James Street and Green Lane in Birkenhead, was officially opened by the Prince of Wales on 20th January 1886 and to the public the following month. It carried 6 million passengers a year in steam-hauled unheated four-wheeled coaches.

The line was then extended to Birkenhead Park on 2nd January 1888 and to Rock Ferry on 15th June 1891, where there were interchange platforms with the Birkenhead Railway. The final extension to Liverpool Central took place on 11th January 1892. Traffic declined due to the dirty environment left by the steam trains and the Mersey Railway was bankrupt. It was rescued by the electric pioneer, George Westinghouse, who electrified the railway and on 3rd May 1903 the nineteen, 3-car electric units of American appearance displaced the steam stock.

In the 1930s the former Wirral Railway lines to West Kirby and New Brighton were electrified, so ending the change from steam traction to the Mersey Railway electric service at Birkenhead Park. On Monday 1st March 1938 the electric service started on the Wirral lines using 3-car electric units built by the LMS at Horwich Works.

In general stock on Merseyrail is in service for many decades. The original Westinghouse American style units were only completely displaced by the LMS 1938 /BR 1956 503 units in 1957. The 503 units themselves were replaced by the 507/508 units in the early 1980s, with these units only now preparing to be displaced by the Stadler Class '777' unit after over four decades.

Mersey Railway side tank 2-6-2 No. 10 *Mersey* of 1887

John Ryan Collection

Mersey Railway 0-6-4T 5 *Cecil Raikes* at Rock Ferry around 1900 and just before the line was electrified. Built by Beyer Peacock of Manchester in 1885 for the opening of the Mersey Railway, the locomotive was used until electrification in 1903. It was then sold to Shipley Collieries in Derbyshire where it saw service until the 1950s. After a period in store it was presented to Liverpool Museums in 1965 but is not currently on display. Although a condensing locomotive, indicated by the large pipe on the tanks, steam propulsion in the tunnels was highly unpopular and electrification, then in its infancy, was the only practical solution to bankruptcy and reversion of traffic to the cleaner ferries. The original signal box is visible in this picture much nearer the platforms. Cecil Raikes himself was chairman of the Mersey Railway and so was present when the two tunnel bores met under the river on 17th January 1884. He took the opportunity to go through the newly formed gap and so was the first person to walk between Liverpool and Birkenhead. *E.C. Lloyd Collection*

No. 6 *Fox* idles away a few moments between services at Birkenhead Central station. Behind is a glimpse of a Mersey Second Class Brake End coach, with a Green Lane destination board on the end. No. 6 was sold to the Alexandra Dock Railway at Newport in South Wales in January 1905, becoming their No. 22. It then went into GWR stock at Grouping in 1923 but although allocated a new number, No. 1344, it was withdrawn in January 1923 without ever carrying it. However, its boiler, being still in good condition, was donated to sister engine GWR No. 1346, ex-Mersey No. 2 *Earl of Chester*. *John Alsop collection*

In low evening light a Class '503' EMU waits to depart for Liverpool Central in the early 1960s. On the adjacent platform a Park Royal DMU is about to leave for Chester.
John Penn Collection

A Class '503' EMU in green livery departs for Liverpool Central from one of Rock Ferry's bay platforms in the 1960s. A further set stands on the centre carriage road. On the adjacent slow lines both the down and up roads have been cleared for trains, indicated by the signal and the banner repeater on the more distant line.
Edgar Richards/Jon Penn Collection

The original Mersey Railway stock was withdrawn between July 1956 and June 1957 and replaced by a second batch of the LMS designed stock; in the last year of service Mersey Railway stock enters Rock Ferry from Liverpool. The new signal box in the foreground was commissioned in 1957 and received an NX Panel to replace its 60 lever frame. It was also necessary to install a small manual 10 lever frame to control the goods lines' semaphore signals, one of which is in the right foreground. Note the lamp man undertaking maintenance. Careful examination of the picture reveals that the right hand arm, the distant signal for Green Lane, is not connected nor a green spectacle glass fitted, as this is a 'fixed distant' signal i.e. permanently displaying caution.

J.F.Davies/Rail Archive Stephenson

The preserved Class '503' EMU, resplendent in LMS maroon livery, passes Rock Ferry signal box with a special train over the reinstated connection on 30th September 1985, to mark the opening of the newly extended electric service to Hooton.

David Southern

When the Mersey Railway was extended from its original terminus of Green Lane to Rock Ferry on 15th June 1891 a significant elevation change had to be overcome and this extension is steeply graded. Descending the incline, a Class '503' EMU approaches Green Lane Station with a Liverpool bound train in the 1970s. A temporary connection had been provided on the opening day so that the royal train of the Prince of Wales (Edward VII) could travel directly into Green Lane station. The Great Western Railway once ran services from Paddington and Ruabon into Liverpool Central via Green Lane, but the 1 in 27 gradient of the Mersey Tunnel was too steep for the Mersey Railway locomotives to handle more than a few coaches. Between 1897 and 1899 there was a brief service of through coaches from Liverpool Central to Folkestone for Paris Nord, well before Eurostar services! *David Southern*

Merseyrail No. 508139 calls at the sub-surface Green Lane station with the inward section of the 16.37 circular train from Ellesmere Port on 5th December 2018. The photograph was taken from the southbound platform which is covered whereas the northbound platform was open and affected by the heavy rainfall – a very strange occurrence. *John Cowlishaw*

BIRKENHEAD CENTRAL

A panorama of Birkenhead Central Station from Mollington Street bridge in the early 1950s illustrates the two covered footbridges originally present at the station. A third footbridge in the foreground is less substantial for staff use only, giving access to the depot and carriage shed hosting three sets of Mersey stock. In front of the signal box, a worker is standing on the fourth rail for return current which was bonded to earth. *E.C. Lloyd Collection*

A similar view taken in 1966 with footbridge now removed hows that the original Mersey stock has now been displaced by the LMS designed Class '503' units. On the platforms the slender gas lights have been replaced by fluorescent strip lights on concrete columns. *Neil Parkhouse*

On a sunny day in the 1950s a Mersey Railway EMU displaying 'British Railways' stands in the bay platform alongside the carriage sheds. The central fourth rail is still in position. In the distance the railway enters into a tunnel under Hamilton Square and shortly will cross under the Haymarket Tunnel of the Birkenhead Extension Railway; an uncommon passing of two railways underground.   *E.C. Lloyd Collection*

Another Mersey Railway EMU enters Birkenhead Central from the Rock Ferry direction bound for Liverpool. Twenty four motor cars and 33 trailer cars were initially constructed of this all American design for the Mersey Railway. Note the unconventional buffering arrangement and behind the well-tended gardens with presumably a staff member excelling in topiary.   *J.F.Davies/Rail Archive Stephenson*

A view of Birkenhead Central around 1905 shows a busy scene with EMUs on both through platforms. The depot had been developed from the old steam shed, which served the whole of the Mersey Railway. At that time the station was still equipped with lower quadrant semaphore signals. *E. Talbot Collection*

The exterior of Birkenhead Central Station is part of a postcard street scene in the 1920s. As well as the impressive car, a Morris 'Bullnose' Oxford, one of the early buses operated by Birkenhead Corporation can be seen. Although the trams endured until 1937, Birkenhead was an early adopter of petrol buses. The large height of the telegraph poles dwarfing the clock tower is noteworthy. This scene has changed almost beyond recognition with the elevated approach roads to the Mersey Tunnel and the relocation of the clock tower. *John Ryan Collection*

A view of Central Station and its environs, possibly on the same day in around 1924, looking in the opposite direction from the previous photograph. The ornate clock tower dominates the scene and two trams are visible opposite the station, with its prominent Mersey Railway sign.
John Ryan Collection

In this later 1950s view the Mersey Railway sign is still there, as it is today, even though British Railways was then long established. People are queuing for the Crosville buses which have replaced the trams. The two different styles of sign can be seen while the numerous chimney pots provide convenient perches for the local pigeons. Note also the post box with its oval sign indicating the direction of the nearest Post Office, in Argyle Street in this case.
E.C. Lloyd Collection

HAMILTON SQUARE

This view, about 1904, is dominated by the hydraulic tower above Mersey Railway's Hamilton Square Station. The tower supplied pressurised water to operate the large lifts taking passengers between the booking hall and the platforms. Also seen on Hamilton Street is the brand new tramcar No. 55 passing a horse drawn cart, whilst a bicycle is being ridden on the pavement. The railway runs directly under the road at this point and the right hand curve of the road in the distance is reflected in the platforms at the station.
John Ryan Collection

This early 1950s view is far less elegant, a corrugated iron garage building has been erected next to the station hence the petrol pumps on the pavement. Although the passenger lifts were converted to electric operation in the 1930s the hydraulic tower was retained and served to advertise the Mersey Railway's 'frequent… electric trains to Liverpool'. The tower and canopy survive to this day. In the right background is the ventilation outlet for the first road tunnel, Queensway, and the chimney to its right is that of the Shore Road Pumping Station of the Mersey Railway.
H C Casserley

The booking hall at Hamilton Square around 1904, with the entrances to the large hydraulic lifts on the left and the central ticket office dominating the picture. Today the scene has changed little even if the tickets are sold from the railway operated shop to the right. *E. Talbot Collection*

The main platforms at Hamilton Square with No. 508132 in the then ubiquitous British Rail corporate livery with the 15.30 West Kirby to Liverpool Central on 30th March 1993. At that time the stations were equipped with chocolate colour moulded plastic seats in the wall lining, these were removed upon refurbishment of the station. The journey of the book now reverses to proceed to Birkenhead North *John Cowlishaw*

As part of the improvements to the Merseyrail network in the 1970s a burrowing junction was made at Hamilton Square so that trains to West Kirby & New Brighton no longer conflicted with northbound trains from Rock Ferry. This involved the construction of a new single platform and No. 508130 enters platform 3 on 1st October 2018 with the westbound section of the 10.13 circular service from New Brighton after traversing the Liverpool loop.

John Cowlishaw

CONWAY PARK

Conway Park is the newest railway station on the Wirral having been opened on 22nd June 1998 by the then leader of the Labour Party, Neil Kinnock. The two photos show construction of the station, which involved inserting a concrete box before removal of the brickwork tunnel, so providing an open air station some 18 metres below ground level.

David Southern

The horizontal struts supporting the walls above the tunnel crown level can be seen on this second photograph.

David Southern

Birkenhead Park station, as the sign says, was where the Mersey Railway from Liverpool met end-on with the Wirral Railway from West Kirby and New Brighton. Although small in scale the station offered services to Liverpool, Hoylake, West Kirby, Wallasey and New Brighton. Dating from 1905 some station staff have come out to pose for the photographer, however the horse and cart in the foreground have been superimposed by the postcard publisher. The station buildings have been replaced but the adjacent terrace and shops survive.
Authors' Collection

Mersey Railway 0-6-4T 4 *Gladstone* is posed around 1900 with its crew at Birkenhead Park. The locomotive was built by Beyer Peacock in 1885 and fitted with condensing apparatus. Upon withdrawal from passenger service the locomotive was retained for use on engineers' trains but being too heavy for this work was shipped to Australia to join three fellow locomotives at a New South Wales colliery. When in operation the condensing steam heated the contents of the tanks so much that these had to be drained upon arrival at Liverpool Central, so adding to the general steamy atmosphere on the railway.
E.C. Lloyd Collection

The Mersey Railway sidings at the Liverpool end of Birkenhead Park station, used for stabling maintenance vehicles, are seen in the mid-1930s. The locomotive is ex-Metropolitan Railway No. 7 *Orion*, built by Beyer Peacock in 1864 and then rebuilt at Neasden in 1921 when it gained its cab. It was bought by the Mersey Railway six years later and remained in service until 1939. The falling gradient on the main lines can be seen along with the portal of Mersey Tunnel (Park Branch) whence the railway commences its subterranean journey to Liverpool.
E.C. Lloyd Collection

In Indian-red lined out livery *Orion* is again seen in its siding, this time looking in the opposite direction towards Park station. The main station building can be seen above the locomotive, while part of the platform and canopy is visible under the bridge. The locomotive was actually the second (hence its number 2) ex-Metropolitan locomotive to carry out engineering duties; its predecessor being their No. 61 of 1884 which was operated by the Mersey Railway from 1907 to 1927. Its successor was an ex-Great Eastern 'J66' 0-6-0T L&NER No. 7297 (later BR No. 68583) which survived until 1958. *E.C.Lloyd Collection*

Damage caused to the rolling stock and carriage sheds at the Liverpool end of Birkenhead Park following the severe air raid on the night of 12th March 1941. Two parachute land mines exploded in the vicinity of the station and in addition to the damage seen, one span of Duke Street Bridge was wrecked resulting in demolition of the station buildings and a huge crater in the middle of the main line tracks. Despite all this, through services to Liverpool were resumed after just five days and the station reopened 11 days after the raid. To safeguard against any further such events, ex-London Transport stock was sent to Merseyside as a contingency. *Birkenhead News Photo Archive*

The bodywork details of Mersey car 29 are seen to advantage as in stands at platform 1 in Birkenhead Park in the 1930s. This platform was served by the Mersey Railway providing a cross-platform interchange with the Wirral Railway using the adjacent platform 2 to the right. Before the extension of services into the Wirral these units were not fitted with air compressors and so the reservoirs to operate the brakes and doors required recharge at both ends of the journey. When services were extended this operation was not possible and compressors were fitted to the stock, as were car heaters.
E.C.Lloyd Collection

In this late 1930s view, rebuilt driving car 30 is at the head of a train of Mersey stock arriving from Liverpool alongside the then new LMS signal box. When built the box had a 60 lever frame but this was replaced by a smaller 25 lever frame in 1972 due to simplification of the track layout. The box closed completely in February 1988 following the removal of all sidings and connections. The train is at the notional junction between the Mersey and LMS railways at the centre of the platforms but both railways frequently crossed into each other's area for shunting before the through running seen here occurred. *E.C.Lloyd Collection*

The seated passenger reading his newspaper is oblivious of car 9 at the head of a train of Mersey stock entering the opposite platform for Liverpool. Although the signal box was built in 1938 by the LMS, in connection with the electrification of the Wirral lines, the Mersey Railway practice of designating all signal boxes by means of a letter was continued, hence H after the name. The photograph is taken after commencement of electric services beyond Birkenhead Park in 1938, as the train is using platform 2 having originated further west in New Brighton (except Sundays) or West Kirby (generally Sundays only). *E.C.Lloyd Collection*

Fowler 'Prairie' tank No. 42 waits to depart from Birkenhead Park with a down train to the Wirral in 1936. To the left hand side of the photograph is the point lock for the crossover on which the fatal accident of 1922 occurred. *J.A.Peden/IRS*

A vintage 0-4-4 No. 5 tank engine on a passenger train at Birkenhead Park station. The coach is of interest with the windows for the guard to see out of the back.
John Ryan Collection

L&NWR Webb 0-6-2T Coal tank No. 7841 in Birkenhead Park station in the 1930s before electrification. The locomotive was withdrawn from Abergavenny in 1948. Note the vintage adverts and the spire of the parish church in the background.
John Ryan Collection

This photograph shows the aftermath of a fatal collision at Birkenhead Park on 6th December 1922, when the 4.00 pm up train from West Kirby came into sidelong collision with the centre of the 4.18 pm down train from Birkenhead Park, which was departing via a crossover connecting the up and down lines. The picture shows Wirral Railway 0-4-4T No. 7 embedded in the side of coach No. 9 on the crossover. One passenger, an invalid in a wheel chair in the brake van, was killed with eight receiving serious injuries and 31 other passengers suffering shock and minor injuries. The accident was found to be the fault of the driver of the up train No. 7, who had passed the protecting signals at danger when entering the station. The method of operation at this time was that the Wirral Railway only used platform 2 of the station, with Mersey Railway only using platform 1 giving many conflicting moves between incoming and outgoing trains. *Birkenhead News Photo Archive*

Another LMS Fowler Class '3P' 2-6-2T No. 18 exits the 71 yard long Cavendish Street tunnel prior to entering Birkenhead Park with an up train about 1937. The lines are not yet electrified as this occurred in the following year but the new elevated cable troughing on the cutting side indicates that this work is imminent. It is interesting to note that the LMS locomotive number sequence started with these somewhat ordinary tank engines whereas the L&NER number sequence commenced with the mighty A4 express locomotives.
E.C.Lloyd Collection

The final view of Birkenhead Park shows the station from Cavendish Street to the west on a sunny 20th May 1956. A Mersey Railway set is in the stabling siding to the left as another 503 unit enters the station heading eastwards towards Liverpool Central. The double island arrangement of the station can clearly be seen.
John Cull/ RCTS Archive CUL1288

BIRKENHEAD NORTH

In July 1956 a Mersey Railway electric unit enters Birkenhead North station with a train to Liverpool Central; the first car has a flat roof whereas the second car has a clerestory roof. The scene is much changed with only the road bridge and platform layout staying the same. The houses have been demolished and the area converted into a very large 'Park & Ride' facility. Under the bridge the former loop leading to additional carriage sheds is visible. *David Kelso*

A Class '503' EMU, No. 28386 a BR 1956 built coach, enters Birkenhead North with a train for Liverpool Central on 27th August 1982. Unusually another EMU is in the third platform, possibly just having come from the depot to enter service for the afternoon peak workings. *Adrian Bodlander*

On 27th August 1982 a West Kirby train boards passengers at Birkenhead North on a sunny afternoon. The footbridge in the background has now been replaced with a more substantial structure incorporating accessible lifts to provide step-free access, and an additional span to connect the station to the large and popular 'Park & Ride' car park to the left. *Adrian Bodlander*

A view of Birkenhead North in the early 1970s from the island platform looking towards Birkenhead Park, with a DMU waiting to depart with a service to Wrexham Central. Following closure of the Seacombe branch in 1960 the Wrexham service was diverted to terminate at New Brighton. From January 1971 Birkenhead North became the terminus until October 1978 when the service was further amended to terminate at Bidston, which is the case today. To the left are two lines, the outer 'Back Road' being curtailed and in the process of being lifted.
David Southern

BR built, Class '508' EMU No. 508117 enters Birkenhead North with a Liverpool bound train on 31st May 1993. Birkenhead North No. 1 signal box was a Wirral Railway design dating from 1888. Both the signal box and the 40 lever tappet frame were supplied by the Railway Signal Company, and survived until the Merseyrail re-signalling scheme of 1994 and transfer of control to Sandhills in Liverpool. *J.A.Peden/IRS*

BIRKENHEAD NORTH LOCOMOTIVE SHED

Birkenhead North engine shed was established by the Wirral Railway on the site of the former Birkenhead Docks station. The station, on Wallasey Bridge Road, was opened by the Hoylake Railway but closed in 1888 becoming a goods station only. Facilities were expanded piecemeal as the railway became busier and eventually included a two road depot, a repair shed and a covered coaling stage. When the LMS took over in 1923, they replaced the Wirral shed with a two-road through building with a partial curved corrugated steel roof and three smoke ventilators. This was the only investment by the LMS until they approved the electrification of the Wirral lines in the 1930s; by the time the shed closed in 1938 it was in a very dilapidated state. The shed was replaced by an electric depot and works, on the site of the former carriage sheds a little further south. In 1965 the site became the location for a coal concentration depot allowing Hinderton Field sidings, near Mollington Street depot, to be closed.

A 1930s view looking west showing Birkenhead North shed in a very poor state, with the long-closed Birkenhead Docks station on the left. The shed roof has suffered severe damage and is absent at this end, with the remains of the rounded roof section at the other end. In the distance beyond the shed, wagons can be seen in the coaling stage. *E.C. Lloyd Collection*

A view of the shed from the opposite side with the curved, corrugated sheeted roof section to the west still in place but somewhat damaged, with the open section beyond. The locomotives visible include L&NWR coal tanks No. 7780 and No. 27664, which indicates the photograph dates after the 1934 renumbering scheme when 20,000 was added to this class. On the further track can be seen one of the two members of the class to receive widened tanks and bunker.
E.C. Lloyd Collection

On the same day but taken in the other direction is the line of locomotives outside the shed including an LMS Class '3F' 0-6-0T *Jinty* No. 7732, a Fowler '3P' 2-6-2T No. 55 and L&NWR coal tank No. 27664 again. The platform in the foreground was part of the original Birkenhead Docks passenger station. It can be seen that the previous photograph must have been taken from the coach roof!   *E.C. Lloyd Collection*

With the poor pitched shed roof of the depot visible, a Fowler 2-6-2T '48' is under the shear legs hoist and an L&NWR coal tank No. 7711 outside the shed. Note the bicycles propped against the shear leg frame.   *E.C. Lloyd Collection*

A general view of Birkenhead north shed with 0-4-4 No. 8 and No. 10 in the rear. The main locomotive shed is to the right.

John Ryan Collection

An L&NWR 'Special Tank' outside Birkenhead North depot in the 1920s. *E.C. Lloyd Collection*

A 1936 interior shot of the shed with a number of Fowler '3P' 2-6-2 tanks and L&NWR coal tanks. *LGRP/NRM*

BIRKENHEAD NORTH ELECTRIC DEPOT

A Mersey Railway electric unit under repair in Birkenhead North depot in the early 1950s, the foreground showing a number of wheel sets with the large gear ring indicating a driven axle. The pipework at the front serves a gas ring for expanding wheel tyres to enable their fitting over the wheel centres.

E.C.Lloyd Collection

An interior view of Mersey Railway car 95 taken in September 1953. Worthy of note are the comfortable leather seats, numerous advertising boards, leather grab straps for standing passengers and the lighting supplied by bare electric bulbs within the taller space. In general these cars found favour in comparison with the 1938 LMS stock but their age lead to the name 'Grandad's Railway' at the end of their lives. Sadly none of this stock was preserved as Car No. 1, although set aside for preservation in 1956, was burned out in a Derby carriage shed on the first day it had moved there for restoration sometime afterwards. By that time no others remained, having being broken up at Horwich Works. *Authors' Collection*

Given its pristine condition a Class '503' EMU No. 28392 appears to have completed its four-yearly overhaul at Horwich Works and is being recommissioned in Birkenhead North depot. The centre door in the cab was fitted after the Liverpool loop line opened (in 1977), to permit evacuation of passengers if the unit failed in the single track tunnel section. This coach was part of the second BR built batch of units from 1956. *David Southern*

Heavy overhauls were carried out at Birkenhead North depot and in 1984 No. 508004 and No. 508027 are seen undergoing bogie changes. The majority of the heavy repairs on these units have for many decades been undertaken in these facilities, as they were superior to those in Liverpool. *David Southern*

Two battery electric units, DB 975179 and DB 977178, are seen inside Birkenhead North depot. These units were converted from Class '501' EMUs (coaches No. 61139 and No. 611136) used on the Euston to Watford Junction services; the work being carried out at Wolverton in 1972. British Railways used them for maintenance work on the Mersey electrified system when the third rail was isolated. These locomotives were used for the removal of spoil from the construction of the tunnels of the Liverpool loop line. *David Southern*

From the bridge to the west of Birkenhead North station in October 1988 track renewal is taking place right outside the depot with excavators loading spent ballast into former mineral wagons, now in engineers' use. On the wagons in the foreground are both old wooden and new concrete sleepered track panels. In the background beyond the spoil train are wagons in Birkenhead North Coal Concentration Depot, served by the Cross-Docks railway. The bracket signal is Birkenhead North No. 1's home signal and can route Liverpool bound trains either side of the station's island platform. Alongside the depot are the battery units seen previously and behind them the de-icing units ABD977347 and 977348, again converted from Class '501' units. For a number of years in the early 1980s Birkenhead's only Class '08' No. 08270, was stabled on this siding necessitating many gricers' visiting this bridge to claim this rare locomotive.

Richard Hambly

By the time this photograph was taken the battery units had been renumbered as DB 977362 and DB 977363, had been converted into de-icing units, and repainted in blue with white edged yellow panels. To further add confusion to the units' renumbering – they were also renumbered 97701 & 97702 for some time. They are seen outside Birkenhead North depot together with Super Sprinter No. 150223 DMU and a Class '08' diesel shunter on adjacent tracks. In the foreground is the River Birkett, a drain running eastwards into the West Float. To the left of the photograph is the area formerly occupied by the original Birkenhead North steam depot of the LMS on the adjacent Cross-Dock Railway, seen earlier.

David Hill

The two journeys described in this book meet at Birkenhead North No. 2, a view of the signal box there looking away from Birkenhead. The main line electrified tracks are on the left whilst on the right are the tracks giving access to Birkenhead North Depot, the coal depot and the docks lines behind the photographer. The electricity substation and cooling towers were part of the short lived (1977-87) Bidston Steelworks which was built on the site of Bidston goods yard, but not rail connected. Birkenhead North No. 2 box dated from 1888 and was built by the Railway Signal Co. for the Wirral Railway. It closed in 1994 as part of the Merseyrail resignalling scheme. In the distance can be seen Bidston East Junction signal box which controlled the main line block section from Birkenhead North No. 1.   At Bidston East Junction the lines split to either West Kirby or New Brighton. *Adrian Bodlander*

In July 1956 the transition from the first to the second stock on the Mersey Railway was in progress. The original American units are seen on the left in their last full year of operation whilst an LMS built 503 unit was about to depart Birkenhead North for Liverpool Central. *David Kelso*

On 5th March 1967 through services from Birkenhead Woodside ceased and two trains ran in commemoration. Preserved No.7029 *Clun Castle*, passes Bebington signal box with the second of the two trains the 'Farewell to the G.W.R. Birmingham - Birkenhead Service' organised by the Stephenson Locomotive Society (Midland Area), heading back to Birmingham Snow Hill.
David Pool

The third-rail electric system was extended on 30th September 1985 from Rock Ferry to Hooton and to mark the occasion one of the Class '503' EMUs, dating from 1938, was restored to its original LMS maroon livery. It is seen at Hooton carrying a commemorative headboard, alongside one of the Class '508's that had replaced the older units
David Southern

In 1995 trams returned to the streets of Birkenhead after an absence of 58 years, when a new heritage line was opened to connect Woodside Ferry with the new transport museum at Taylor Street, a distance of ¾ of a mile. Blackpool Council operated the trams on behalf of Wirral Council as they had the necessary safety licence. Wirral finally took over running the service in 2005 but found the operation was not financially viable. In 2014 it was agreed that operation be handed over to the Merseyside Tramway Preservation Society and the service is now operated entirely by volunteers. The photo shows tram 69 passing through the old dock entrance in around 2000 alongside one of the restored police huts. The tram is running directly above the Mersey Rail Tunnel at this point. Tram 69 is one of two trams built in Hong Kong especially for this line. A number of preserved trams from Birkenhead, Wallasey and Liverpool are also available for service.

Harry Leadbetter